THE LUSHAI EXPEDITION

1871—1872

R. G. WOODTHORPE
LIEUT. ROYAL ENGINEERS

VONOLEL'S TOMB

The Naval & Military Press Ltd

❖

Reproduced by kind permission of the Central Library,
Royal Military Academy, Sandhurst

Published by
The Naval & Military Press Ltd
Unit 10, Ridgewood Industrial Park,
Uckfield, East Sussex,
TN22 5QE England
Tel: +44 (0) 1825 749494
Fax: +44 (0) 1825 765701
www.naval-military-press.com

© The Naval & Military Press Ltd 2004

A GROUP:—LUSHAI—POI—LUSHAI—SOKTÉ.

CONTENTS.

CHAPTER I.

THE NORTH EASTERN FRONTIER—HISTORICAL RETROSPECT—POLICY OF CONCILIATION—FORMER EXPEDITIONS—ANNEXATION OF CACHAR PROPER—TEA-GARDENS—THE KOOKIE TRIBE—FIRST APPEARANCE OF THE LUSHAIS—CHIEF LALAL—HIS FOUR SONS—RAIDS IN SYLHET, CACHAR, &C.—COLONEL LISTER'S EXPEDITION.   1

CHAPTER II.

GNURSHAILON'S RAID — CAPTAIN STEWART — TREATY WITH SUKPILAL—RENEWAL OF COMPLICATIONS—CAPTIVES DETAINED—REPEATED INROADS OF THE LUSHAI—MR. BAKER'S EXPEDITION—HIS DESCRIPTION OF THE COUNTRY—DEATHS OF SOME OF THE CHIEFS—ATTACKS ON VARIOUS TEA-GARDENS   19

CHAPTER III.

EXPEDITION OF 1871—COLONEL RABAN'S RECOMMENDATIONS—
GENERAL BOURCHIER—THE ROUTE—RELATIONS WITH THE
RAJAH OF MUNIPUR—BURMESE INVASIONS—VICISSITUDES
OF MUNIPUR—MAJOR-GENERAL NUTHALL—INROADS OF
THE EASTERN LUSHAI CHIEFS   37

CHAPTER IV.

THE TOPOGRAPHICAL SURVEY OF INDIA—COOLIES—CACHAR—
MUNIPUR HORSE-DEALERS — HOCKEY-PLAYERS — UNCOM-
FORTABLE MODE OF RIDING—PRESENT FOR A CHIEF—TEA-
GARDENS—NATIVE IDOLS—THE MONIERKHAL STOCKADE—
RUMOURS OF A THREATENED ATTACK — CURIOUS DIS-
COVERY   50

CHAPTER V.

THE LUSHAIS—CHARACTERISTICS OF THREE PRINCIPAL TRIBES
—FEATURES AND COMPLEXION—MUSCULAR STRENGTH—IN-
TELLECTUAL APTITUDE—COSTUME—PERSONAL ADORNMENT—
A LUSHAI EXQUISITE — PRACTICE OF SMOKING — TOBACCO
WATER—WEAPONS—GUNPOWDER 69

CHAPTER VI.

LUSHAI VILLAGES—CONSTRUCTION OF THE HOUSES—INTERNAL
ARRANGEMENTS — WINDOWS — STOCKADES—NATIVE WINE —
BASKET-MAKING — DOMESTIC ANIMALS — CURIOUS MACHINE
FOR ENTRAPPING GAME — AGRICULTURAL OPERATIONS —
MUSICAL INSTRUMENTS—A SMITH'S FORGE .   .   81

CHAPTER VII.

LEFT COLUMN OF THE EXPEDITION—THE COMMISSARIAT DE-
PARTMENT—POLITICAL OFFICER—SILCHAR—THE ARTILLERY
AND SAPPERS—FIRST CASUALTY OF THE CAMPAIGN—ROUTE
FROM SILCHAR TO MYNADHUR — APPEARANCE OF THE
COUNTRY—DIFFICULTIES OF THE MARCH . . 95

CHAPTER VIII.

MYNADHUR—THE TELEGRAPH—A DAILY POST ESTABLISHED—
ROUTE TO TIPAI MUKH—SCENERY ON THE BARAK—TRIAL
OF ELEPHANTS — ENCAMPMENT — THE GOORKHAS—VARIOUS
STATIONS—TIPAI MUKH – BRIDGE BUILT BY KOOKIES—A
NATIVE SAPPER—THE COMMISSARIAT FLEET OF BOATS—A
LUSHAI IDEA 109

CHAPTER IX.

VILLAGE SITES—RUMOURS—DARPONG—THE SENVONG RANGE—
FIRST VIEW OF THE LUSHAI COUNTRY—EXTRAORDINARY HILL
—SYMBOLIC WARNINGS TO THE TROOPS—WEIR FOR CATCHING
FISH—ATTEMPTS TO STOP THE ADVANCE—A SKIRMISH—
CHRISTMAS DAY. 127

CHAPTER X.

TEMPORARY CESSATION OF HOSTILITIES—THE LUSHAI AC-
COUNT OF THE KHOLEL AFFAIR—DIFFICULTY OF COMMUNI-
CATING WITH THE NATIVES—A GUIDE FOR THE SURVEY
OFFICERS—THE MUNIPUR CONTINGENT—POIBOI'S PRESENTS—
EVENTS AT TIPAI MUKH—LUSHAI ATTACK. . . 145

CHAPTER XI.

PROGRESS OF THE HEAD-QUARTERS—AT WORK ON THE ROAD—
A DESERTED VILLAGE—UNCOMFORTABLE NIGHT—AN EMIS-
SARY FROM SUKPILAL—THE CAMP AT CHEPUI—POIBOIS—
THE SENIVAI—GUARD VILLAGES—THE KHOLEL RANGE   163

CHAPTER XII.

SITE OF THE VILLAGE OF KHOLEL—VOUPILAL'S TOMB—ENGLOOM
—THE HEAD-MAN OF CHEPUI—SWEARING ETERNAL FRIEND-
SHIP — ARTISTIC JUDGMENT — DISTRIBUTION OF · TROOPS—
MIDNIGHT PARLEYS—ATTEMPTED DECEPTION—LUSHAI WINE
APPRECIATED—VILLAGE LIFE.   177

CHAPTER XIII.

MORE SYMBOLIC WARNINGS—DESIGNS OF THE LUSHAI CHIEFS—
RECONNOITERING—DARPONG—ORDER OF MARCH—FIGHT WITH
THE LUSHAIS — SMALL BUT FORMIDABLE STOCKADE — THE
LUSHAIS TAKEN IN FLANK—CASUALTIES—NARROW ESCAPE
OF THE GENERAL   195

CHAPTER XIV.

COUNCIL OF THE CHIEFS—OUR WEAK POINT—KUNGNUNG—THE
LENGTENG RANGE — ADVANCE OF THE TROOPS — A STRONG
STOCKADE—A DETOUR—ARTILLERY PRACTICE—EFFECT OF
SHELLS—STRIKING SCENE—A CURIOUS GRAVE   .   , 211

CHAPTER XV.

TELEGRAM FROM CACHAR—RESCUE OF MARY WINCHESTER—
FIGHT OF LUSHAIS AND CLASSIS — ESCAPE OF A LUSHAI
PRISONER—A DISTURBER OF THE CAMP—TOUCHING SCENE—
THE SAIVAR—POIBOI'S STRONGHOLD—A CURIOUS HUNT—
ALARM OF FIRE—A THOUGHTFUL BOY. . . . 227

CHAPTER XVI.

THE TROOPS ENCAMPED—LALBOORA'S GATE—A VISIT TO NATIVE
VILLAGERS—TELESCOPES—DIFFICULTY OF OBTAINING PHOTO-
GRAPHS—CAPTIVES PLACED UNDER OUR PROTECTION—THE
MUNIPUR CONTINGENT — POIBOI'S VACILLATION — LUSHAI
FORTIFICATIONS—A LUSHAI TODTLEBEN . . . 245

CHAPTER XVII.

THE TRUE POIBOI—DEFENCES OF THE VILLAGE OF TULCHENG—
SCARCITY OF WATER—ROMANTIC STORY OF TWO CHILDREN—
VALLEY OF THE LUI-TAO—HEAVY FIRING HEARD—LETTER-
WRITING UNDER DIFFICULTIES—INGENIOUSLY CONSTRUCTED
GATE 263

CHAPTER XVIII.

VONOLEL'S VILLAGE—VONOLEL'S TOMB – PLEASING TRAIT IN A
DOCTOR—BUILDING OPERATIONS—CONDITIONS OF PEACE—
FRATERNISING—MADAME RACHEL'S WIDELY SPREAD REPU-
TATION—OUR INTERCOURSE WITH THE LUSHAIS—LIGHTING
PIPES—EXPERIMENTS WITH THE BURNING GLASS . 279

CHAPTER XIX.

DELIVERY OF THE FINE—DIFFICULTY IN COLLECTING THE MUSKETS—ACCEPTABLE CHANGE OF DIET—THE COMMISSA-RIAT — AUSTRALIAN MUTTON — A COOLIE TRICK — LUSHAI RAIDS—THE TRAGEDY AT BLAIR—RETURN MARCH   . 295

CHAPTER XX.

WITHDRAWAL OF THE TROOPS—SECOND HALT—DISTRIBUTION OF PRESENTS—DARPONG'S WATCH—CABULI FRUIT-SELLERS —LUSHAI ENTERTAINMENT—APPEARANCE OF THE COUNTRY —DAK ARRANGEMENTS—THE RESCUED CAPTIVES—COOLIE ENTERTAINMENTS—RETURN TO TIPAI MUKH—PROFITABLE COMMERCE   307

CHAPTER XXI.

HARDSHIPS OF THE CAMPAIGN—DEATH OF TWO OFFICERS— INDISPOSITION OF THE GENERAL—RAVAGES OF CHOLERA —THE MUNIPUR CONTINGENT—CONFERENCE—PRECAUTIONS AGAINST TREACHERY—SEIZURE OF CHIEFS—FALSE PRE-DICTION—ORDER TO THE TROOPS—CONCLUDING REMARKS 321

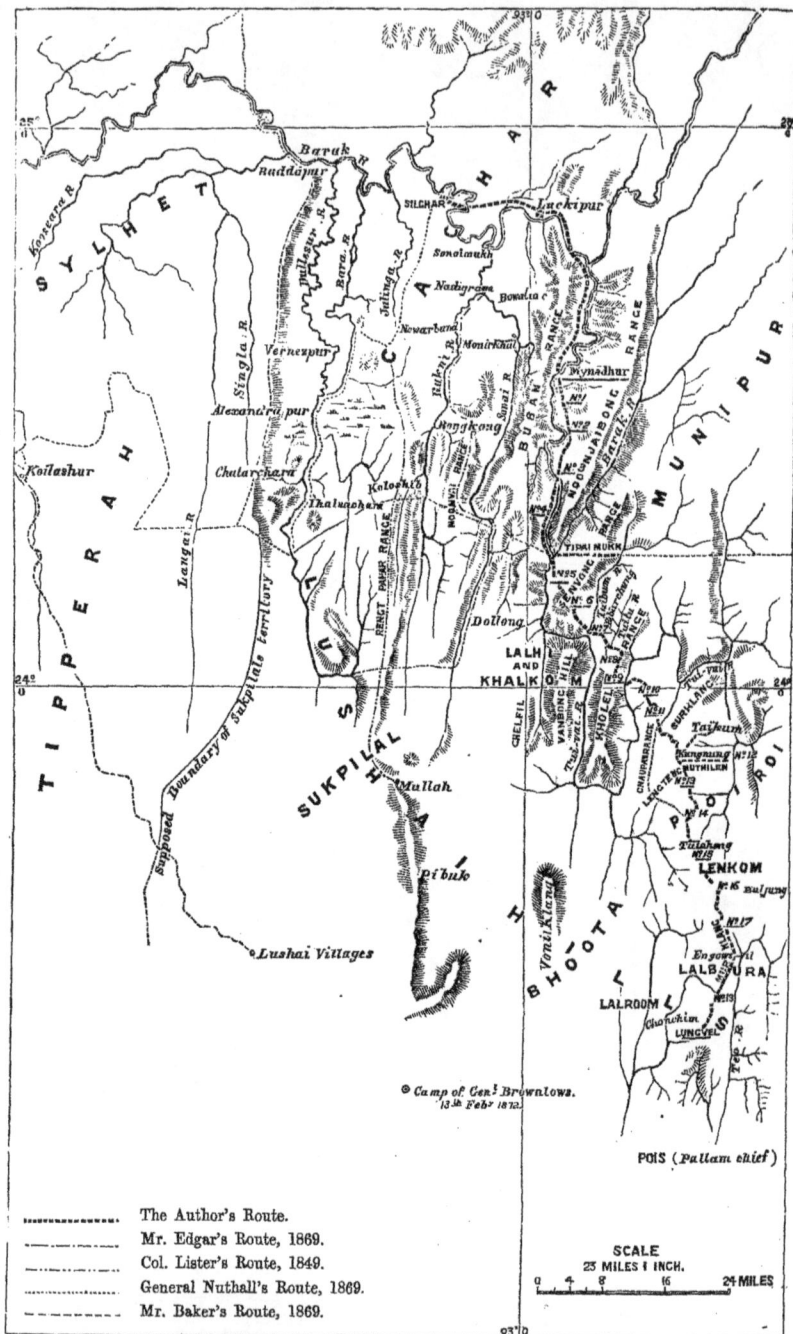

MAP showing the country passed through by the LEFT COLUMN OF THE LUSHAI EXPEDITIONARY FORCE, 1871-72, and the Routes taken in former Expeditions.

CHAPTER I.

THE NORTH-EASTERN FRONTIER—HISTORICAL RETROSPECT—
POLICY OF CONCILIATION—FORMER EXPEDITIONS—ANNEXA-
TION OF CACHAR PROPER—TEA-GARDENS—THE KOOKIE TRIBE
—FIRST APPEARANCE OF THE LUSHAIS—CHIEF LALAL—HIS
FOUR SONS—RAIDS IN SYLHET, CACHAR, &C.—COLONEL
LISTER'S EXPEDITION.

CHAPTER I.

THE North-eastern frontier of India has ever been a fruitful source of trouble and expense to the Government of this Empire. The history of each district on this frontier, whether prior or subsequent to its annexation as a portion of British territory, is almost the same. Bordered by, or forming part of hill districts, inhabited by fierce and predatory tribes for ever making raids on their neighbours' villages, burning and plundering them, and carrying off the inhabitants—it was not to be supposed that those under our protection should escape.

When, in consequence of outrages on British subjects, the Indian Government has been forced

B 2

to take steps for their protection, its policy towards the offenders has generally been one of conciliation rather than retaliation. The success which has usually followed the adoption of this policy seems to be the best argument in its favour.

While, at the same time, establishing and maintaining frontier guards to check any outrage as far as possible, annual payments are made to the chiefs of tribes, or, in the case of a democracy to the community—not in order to enable them to organize among themselves a force for the preservation of order, but that the well-disposed among them may influence the more turbulent spirits to the prevention of any infringement of the treaties or agreements made with them on granting the annual allowances.

On the annexation of a district, the rights of the Hillmen are always scrupulously respected, any losses they sustain being made good to them; and by opening up fresh avenues of trade and commerce to them, they are led to see that a peaceable attitude towards us is more profitable for themselves than one of aggression.

The allowances to those over whom we do not assume government, are supposed, in the words of the Indian Government itself, " to be sufficient to compensate the tribes, in their own estimation, for the advantage they might gain by the occasional plunder of a border village—an advantage which they well know is materially qualified by the risk of reprisals."

It appears that in the last century some fierce tribes, who had been the terror of the surrounding country, and whom successive military expeditions had failed to subdue, were induced by an annual payment, conditional on good conduct, to become quiet and peaceable neighbours.

" What is of the utmost importance in dealing with uncivilized tribes is patience. No one supposes that their civilization is to be effected in a few years, and no one expects that, in endeavouring to conciliate them, the Government will not meet with occasional disappointment; but the policy is none the less on this account sound and intelligible."

Thus spoke Government in 1865, and the

policy thus indicated will be carried out with reference to the Lushais. Of course, a policy of conciliation would be ineffectual, without impressing on the tribes a conviction of our power to punish them if necessary; and in many cases, as in the present instance, we have been obliged to do so before adopting this policy of peace.

The Government does not wish to exterminate these frontier tribes, but by converting them into our allies to raise a barrier between our frontier districts and other more distant races. Supposing a tribe to be utterly crushed or exterminated, we should find ourselves no better off than before—probably much worse, having merely removed obstacles to the assaults of a fiercer and more formidable foe, whose very remoteness would render it difficult for us to conciliate or punish him.

I do not propose to enter into an account of the raids or consequent expeditions which have been made at various times in the different districts of our North-eastern frontier, but confine myself to a brief narrative of those which have taken place in Cachar since its annexation; as to avenge the late raids there, and by securing the peace of that frontier, to enable the tea-planters, on Government grants, and their labourers, to follow their occupation in safety, were the objects proposed by Government to the Commanders of the Lushai Expedition of 1871-72.

The district of Cachar Proper, as it is called, was annexed to the British dominions about 1832, after the death of its legitimate rajah, Gobind Chundra. It is bounded on the north by the hills known as the North Cachar Hills; on the west by the British district of Sylhet; on the east by the western bank of the Jiri River to its junction with the Barak, near Luckipur, and thence by the western bank of the Barak as far as Tipai Mukh, where a stone pillar, erected by the Revenue Survey, marks the tri-junction of Munipur, Cachar, and the Lushai hillls. The coast boundary line on the south is still rather indefinite.

The whole of the Northern half of Cachar is more or less under cultivation at present, and well populated. The country is tolerably level, broken here and there by low tilas (small hills) of about two hundred feet in height, and intersected by the Sonai, Rukni, and Dullesur rivers, which, rising in the southern hills, flow through Cachar to join the Barak. Large bheels, or swamps, high grass jungle, and bad roads, however, render communication between the different gardens a matter of some difficulty.

To the East rises the great Buban range, which, commencing a little south of Luckipur, and running nearly parallel to the general course of the Barak towards the southern boundary of Cachar, attains at several points an elevation of four thousand feet, and is clothed throughout with thick forest jungle.

A few of the Lushai ranges rise in the south of Cachar. These are the Noonvai and Rengtipahar, and on the western boundary the lofty range of the Chatarchara; but between these the whole of South Cachar is a succession of dangerous swamps and low broken ranges, covered with the densest jungle.

The tea-gardens, which were originally confined to the northern part of the district, have of late years been sweeping further and further south, as enterprising individuals have been found to take grants from Government for the cultivation of the tea-plant.

These isolated gardens, small clearings in the heart of the jungles, possessing few means of communication with the outer world, offer peculiar temptations to raiders ; especially as in the bungalows of many of the planters are kept large stands of ancient guns, to inspire confidence in the labourers in the gardens, but to obtain possession of which the Lushais would think few efforts and sacrifices too great; and it is in these gardens, as we shall see, that the principal outrages have of late years been committed.

The lofty hills to the south of Munipur, Cachar, and a portion of the territory to the south-west of Cachar, known as Independent or Hill Tipperah, have been held by various families of the Kookie tribe from the earliest times of which we have any record.

The name Kookie has been given to this great tribe, as Mr. Edgar tells us, by the Bengalis, and is not recognized by the Hillmen themselves. He says:—

" I have never found any trace of a common name for the tribe among them, although they seem to consider different families as belonging to a single group, which is certainly coextensive with what we call the Kookie tribe."

The principal families with whom we first came in contact, were the Tangune, Chausels, Ladoé, and Poitoo Kookies. All authorities agree in stating that from a very early period, the tribes to the south have been gradually driving one another in a northern direction; formerly the Buban Hills and a portion of South Cachar were occupied by some members of a race called Nagas; but these were obliged, by the Tangunes, to withdraw to the North Cachar hills.

The Tangunes, occupying their ground, were in their turn dispossessed and driven to the northern hills by the Chausels and Ladoés. These have likewise been compelled to retire northward by the Lushais.

The Poitoo Kookies inhabited the hills on each side of the valley of the Gootur river, and were supposed to be more or less subject to the Rajah of Tipperah. The relations existing between the Poitoo chief and the Rajah were, however, repudiated on occasion by each.

The Lushais first appeared on the scene about the year 1840, the first chief of whom we had any knowledge being Lalal; from whom are descended the chiefs who have lately been the cause of so much anxiety to the Indian Government.

He had four sons. Of these, when we first hear of them, Mongpir was struggling in the west against the Poitoos, to establish himself on the Chatarchara range; Lalingvoom was ruling the villages south of the hill known as Peak Z, in the Great Trigonometrical Survey of India; while Lalsavoong was striving with the Ladoés in the east for possession of the Chumfai valley and range to the north of it.

In 1844, an attack was made on a village of Sylhet by some Poitoo Kookies, under a chief named Lalchokla, when twenty human heads and six live captives were carried off. It was said that the raid was made to procure heads to bury with a chief who had lately died.

The Rajah of Tipperah was called upon by the Government to assist in punishing Lalchokla, and recovering the captives; but as his co-operation was very unsatisfactory, and the steps he took manifestly inadequate to accomplish their object, a party of troops, under Captain Black-wood, proceeded viâ Koilashur, on the 1st of December, to attack Lalchokla's village.

Assisted by a Kookie chief, our troops ar-rived at the village and surrounded it, and by destroying the grain in the country around, the Poitoo chief was speedily reduced to submission, and surrendered on the 4th. He confessed to the raid, but professed ignorance of the fact that it had been made on British subjects. This plea of ignorance was not admitted, and he was eventually transported for life.

It has been said that one of the conditions of his surrender was that his life would be spared. This he took to mean a free pardon; consequently the Kookies looked upon his transportation as a breach of faith on our part. This is alleged as one reason for the difficulty experienced during the late Expedition in inducing chiefs to come in personally to make their submission.

We next hear, in November, 1849, of some raids made simultaneously in Sylhet, Tipperah, and Cachar. The raid in the latter district was made by Lalingvoom's son, Mora, on some Ladoé villages not far from the station; and to punish these outrages an Expedition was organized, and the command entrusted to Colonel Lister, Political Agent in the Khasia Hills, and Commandant of the Sylhet Light Infantry.

The Expedition started from Cachar on the 4th of January, 1850, and marching nearly due south, on the 14th, arrived at the large village of Mora or Moolla, which Colonel Lister at once attacked and destroyed. Most of the inhabitants managed to escape, but about four hundred captives were released; and proofs were found identifying the villagers with the Sylhet raiders. Colonel Lister remained a short time on the

range, but deeming his force too small for any
further operations, he returned to Cachar on
the 23rd.

The Lushais, during his stay, annoyed him
by firing into his camp, endeavouring to cut
off his communications, and when he retired,
followed him, killing any straggling coolies they
came across.

Colonel Lister considered that, in order to
make a permanent impression on the tribes, a
force of not less than three thousand men would
be required, "and to command their villages,
a road would have to be carried into the heart
of the country, along one of the ridges of hills
which ran north and south. As a protective
measure, the establishment of armed outposts
of friendly Kookies along the frontier was
advocated."

This question of opening a road through from
end to end of the country, is again being urged
upon Government as one of the first things
necessary, in order to reap permanent advantages from the success of this last expedition
of 1871-72.

Colonel Lister also recommended the formation of a Kookie levy to be employed as scouts in the southern jungles, to collect information concerning the Lushais, and the events which were occurring on the other side of our frontier, as well as to keep a watch over the Kookies in our own territory and Munipur.

Government approved of all Colonel Lister's recommendations, and suggested opening up negotiations with the Lushai Chief. The Kookie levy was raised in June, 1850.

The special objects for which it was raised seem to have soon been lost sight of, as we find the establishment of the Kookie scouts abolished in 1860, and the levy handed over to the police. In the endeavour to make them well drilled soldiers, they gradually lost their special qualifications as scouts and trackers, and the Kookie constables who accompanied the left column, proved utterly useless for the work which should have been theirs, and for which they were expressly intended.

The consequence of the abolition of a body of scouts was the increasing ignorance on the part of the authorities of what was going on among the Kookies and Lushais—for information concerning whom they were obliged to rely upon one man, a Kookie, named Maujihow, who, as it has since been discovered, deceived them on several important occasions.

· The results, nevertheless, of Colonel Lister's Expedition were very great, as no raids occurred either in Sylhet or Cachar till 1862; and in the meantime negotiations had been conducted between the Cachar authorities and the Lushai chiefs.

In October, 1850, five Lushai chiefs sent deputies into Cachar with friendly overtures to the Superintendent, who sent a party down to meet the Lushais. This party returned, accompanied by the Muntri (ambassador) of Sukpilal, the great chief of the Western Lushais.

When the Lushais returned to their own country, the Superintendent sent an emissary with them, with friendly messages to the chief, and assurances that if he went into Cachar he should not be injured nor detained.

Sukpilal was supposed to have visited Cachar

in December, but Mr. Edgar thinks, as this visit
is denied by all the Kookies, that finding that
presents would only be given to Sukpilal himself
some one was got to personate that chief. The
result, however, was the establishment of trading
relations between the natives of Hyrapandy and
the Lushais.

In 1855, Sukpilal sent in to the Superintendent for assistance against some neighbouring chiefs. Government, however, refused to
interfere in the quarrels of tribes living beyond
our frontier.

Mora also sent in a deputation for help to
secure the exchange of prisoners between himself
and the Munipuris, on whom some raids had been
committed; and this help we were ready to
afford him.

CHAPTER II.

GNURSHAILON'S RAID — CAPTAIN STEWART — TREATY WITH
SUKPILAL — RENEWAL OF COMPLICATIONS — CAPTIVES DE-
TAINED—REPEATED INROADS OF THE LUSHAI—MR. BAKER'S
EXPEDITION—HIS DESCRIPTION OF THE COUNTRY—DEATHS
OF SOME OF THE CHIEFS — ATTACKS ON VARIOUS TEA-
GARDENS.

CHAPTER II.

SINCE this time nothing seems to have occurred till January, 1862, when three villages were plundered and burnt in the neighbourhood of Adumpur, and evidence went to show that the leader in this outrage was Gnurshailon, son of Lalchokla, who had married a sister of Sukpilal.

No steps were taken by Government till 1864, when four captives made their escape from Cachar, and from their statements it appeared that Sukpilal, and two other Poitoo chiefs, Rungboom and Lalltolien, were also implicated, and that many of the captives were living at that time in the villages of these chiefs.

The local authorities desired an Expedition

to be sent against them, but it was feared that this might bring down the Kookies on the tea-gardens, which are rapidly spreading south, and, before attempting force, Captain Stewart, the Deputy Commissioner was desired to open negotiations with Sukpilal to induce him to give up the captives in his possession.

The latter sent his muntri to Captain Stewart. He admitted his guilt in the Adumpur matter, but said that some of the captives had been sold to the Pois, a powerful tribe to the south-east of Sukpilal's territory.

Captain Stewart required the chief to come to him, bringing with him the captives, and swear friendship, on doing which he would receive fifty rupees a month, subject to a small annual tribute of certain specified articles.

The muntri said that Sukpilal's son should go in, as the chief was too ill to move, and agreed to the other conditions.

About the same time Captain Stewart concluded a similar treaty with Voupilal, son of Mora, who had succeeded his father as chief of the Kholal villages, whither the latter had removed after the destruction of his village by Colonel Lister in 1850.

A new rajah had in the meantime assumed the reigns of government in Tipperah, and to strengthen his position he offered to do all in his power to seize Gnurshailon and Sukpilal. His offer was, however, refused, as the negotiation with the latter seemed to promise fairly.

In December, 1865, however, it was reported that Sukpilal had not given up the captives, and no satisfactory reason being given for this non-compliance with the terms of his agreement, an Expedition was organised to compel their release.

The rainy season setting in before it could start, the operations were postponed. During the rains, Captain Stewart was employed in inquiring into the accessibility and position of Sukpilal's villages. He considered that no approach could be made from the Chittagong side (this has since been proved to be a mistaken notion), and that at least four hundred men should be sent from Cachar. The idea of an Expedition was then abandoned.

Shortly after Sukpilal opened negotiations again, by sending in the annual presents, but no captives; but after much trouble four were at length sent in. Gnurshailon, it was said, through whom Sukpilal obtained muskets from Tipperah, prevented his sending in the others. Many of the captives were said to be married to Lushais, and unwilling to leave them. There was probably some truth in this statement, as we shall see from an incident which occurred during the late Expedition.

Towards the close of 1868, attacks were made on some Naga villages in Munipur, and Rungboom's villages in Hill Tipperah. In the latter Sukpilal was supposed to be concerned; and at the same time the tea-gardens in South Cachar were threatened.

On the 10th January, 1869, the Lushais, under a chief named Lalroom, Voupilal's brother-in-law, burnt the tea-garden of Nowarbund and killed some of the coolies, and another party under Deouti, on the 14th, attacked the Monir-khal garden, where there was a stockade and a police-guard; he succeeded in destroying the buildings and plundering the garden.

Early in February an attack was made on the Kala Naga stockade by Lushais, under Lenkom. The stockade was taken, and a Munipur officer and some Sepoys killed.

Voupilal and Sukpilal were suspected from the first, though the actual raiders were not discovered till afterwards, and an attempt was made to punish them.

A large Expedition was set on foot, consisting of two forces of Military and Police, one intended to proceed up the Sonai to punish Voupilal, the other to reach Sukpilal by the Dullesur River. The Rajah of Munipur was also to have co-operated from his side.

These plans were altered considerably, and the Expedition was unsuccessful. The plan of operations to be carried out was this :—Simultaneously with the advance of the columns from Cachar, one composed principally of police under Mr. Baker, Deputy Inspector-General, was to march on Sukpilal from Koilashur through Rungboom's villages.

The Cachar column, under General Nuthall, which proceeded up the Dullesur, was obliged

by rain, to turn back, before reaching the
enemy's country, having only proceeded three
marches from the furthest tea-garden.

Mr. Baker, whose orders were to effect a
junction with the Dullesur column at Sukpilal's
villages if possible, or if not to return by
the shortest route to Sylhet, marched from
Koilashur towards the middle of February.
Notwithstanding the failure of the Tipperah
Rajah's Minister to assist him with carriage
and food, in accordance with the orders received from the Rajah, notwithstanding also
the heavy rains which delayed him several
days, Mr. Baker succeeded in reaching the
Lushai villages.

On the way there, he passed the place
where Rungboom's people had been treacher-
ously killed by Lushais in December, and saw
eleven skeletons in one spot. Rungboom himself had escaped, but was pursued by the
Lushais, who burnt his villages. They were
repulsed by the police of the Adumpur
guard, and compelled to retire, having killed
about eighty or ninety persons.

On the 17th March, Mr. Baker's column
arrived in sight of the Lushai villages, and
there being no signs of the approach of that
under General Nuthall, he determined, after
consultation with his officers, to hold on for
another day, and in the meantime to make a
reconnaissance, to try to pick up some food,
there being none then in camp.

A brush with Lushais took place, and our
men returned to camp in the evening. It
being evident that the Dullesur column had not
advanced for some reason or other, and that
with the small force at his disposal, he could
not hope to cope successfully with the whole
tribe, Mr. Baker determined to fall back on
the Depot in rear, and the retreat commenced the next day.

On the 21st, a telegram from Cachar informed
him that General Nuthall and his column were
back in Cachar, so there was nothing to do
but to return with all speed to Sylhet.

Mr. Baker describes the country passed
through by his column, thus :—

" The country traversed by us was alto-

gether hilly, we passed no morasses, and excepting the forest lying between the Karruntah
range and the banks of the Deo, the country
was found to be high, dry, and free from
malaria at this season.

" Small streams were met with at the bases
of all the higher hills, and occasionally springs
on the hill-sides not far from the tops of
the ridges. The rivers crossed, the Munneo,
Deo, Pakwa, &c., were from twenty to thirty
yards wide, and about two or three feet
deep, having firm sandy beds, easily forded;
but in the rainy season they must become
exceedingly deep and rapid streams.

" Judging by their high steep banks, they are
liable to great rises and sudden falls, and
they are much blocked up with fallen timbers.
On some of the ranges are sites of old Kookie
villages, now overgrown with high grass, but
there are still some fine trees left, among
them a few lemon.

" Game seemed to be abundant along the
course of the rivers. Elephants are extremely
numerous in these valleys, and there are

deer, wild hogs, porcupines, and in the Langai valley rhinoceros are said to be found.

" The principal ranges of hills run north and south, but between these the smaller ranges are innumerable; in fact, the entire country is a jumble of hills. The main features are, therefore, mountain ranges of one thousand to two thousand feet in height, at intervals of ten or twelve miles, trending north and south; of confused lines of hills and spurs running down to the bottom of these intervening spaces; and lastly of deep and narrow streams flowing along the lowest levels from north to south, over sandy or rocky beds, and in very winding courses, often under high and precipitous banks. This very well describes the character also of the country south and west of Tipai Mukh."

Mr. Baker submitted among others the following suggestions as the results of his experience, and as likely to be useful in the case of a future expedition. Several of these were adopted, and it would have been better if some of the others had also been followed.

"In expeditions of this nature the carriage of supplies and the clearing of a sufficiently convenient path, are of course, the chief points to be alluded to. I believe the Lushais will fight on their own ground, and in their own desultory manner . . . . I would recommend—

"For carriage :

"Boats to the furthest point they can go up in November and December, afterwards coolies and elephants.

"To open roads :

"A company of pioneers, and attached to them a body of one hundred Kookie jungle-cutters.

*   *   *   *

"Half a battery of mountain guns, carried on *mules in preference to elephants*, would prove serviceable, and would save time and reduce the casualties in taking defended stockades.

"Every man in the force should be supplied with a ' kookrie,' a ' dao,' a water-bottle, and havresack capable of containing his ' shalee,' ' lotah,' and some food.

"Coolies properly organised and officered would prove more reliable than elephants, but a score or two of the latter would be useful. No tents should be allowed for either men or officers, and their personal baggage reduced to a minimum.

"The columns prepared in good time, say in November, should move steadily, if slowly, making the marches as little trying as possible."

The portion of the force which went up the Sonai with Mr. Edgar got to one of Voupilal's villages, the headman of which, with his mother, went, and offered to make submission, declaring that Voupilal, who had lately died, had taken no part in the raid on Munipur, which had been made by Poiboi alone. They gave Mr. Edgar very accurate information about the other raids, and promised to do what they could to induce the Eastern chiefs to come to terms. The force then returned to Cachar.

The Munipur Contingent was prevented by stress of weather from doing anything, and thus ended this Expedition, from which such great results had been anticipated.

In the next raids, which took place in the cold
weather following, some new Lushai chiefs appeared, and it will be necessary just to look
back for a little at the changes which had taken
place among the principal families.

Voupilal had died in 1869, and his people are
divided in their allegiance between his mother
and his widow. The former lives at Dollong,
the latter on Vanbong Hill, whither the villagers removed from Kholel on the death of
Voupilal. The widow claims the regency on behalf
of her infant son Lalhi. Khalkom, Sukpilal's
son, has moved his village across the Sonai to
the ridge on which Dollong is situated, and
supports the mother against the widow, who is
assisted by her brother Poiboi.

Lalsavoong having made himself master of
the Chumfai Valley and neighbourhood, died
about 1849, leaving three sons who became
powerful chiefs, of these Vonolel proved himself
the most powerful and ablest of all the Lushais;
and in his constant struggles with neighbouring
tribes, was generally successful.

He fought with the Pois and carried off large

numbers, whom he settled in separate villages,
or among his own people. He pursued the same
policy with the Soktés, a powerful tribe in the
East, under Kamlion, the chief of Molbhem.
He was succeeded on his death a few years ago
by his young son Lalboora.

Another son of Lalsavoong was Lalpoong,
who had become head of the villages of Chelam
and the others now belonging to Poiboi, his
son, who is still a mere boy.

In December, 1870, Mr. Edgar went down to
see Sukpilal, and settled finally the boundary
fixed provisionally the year before. After seeing
this chief, Mr. Edgar had great difficulty in
returning, being without provisions, and receiving no tidings as to the boats which were
to have been sent down the Sonai, he was
obliged to encamp for some time, while he sent
men to get information as to his supplies, and
the temper of the neighbouring Lushais. Sukpilal's people treated him well, taking him such
provisions as they could, till the arrival of a
small party of the 44th, under Captain Lightfoot,
enabled him to return to Cachar.

During his stay in the country, he received tidings of intended raids on Cachar, which at the time he did not believe, though he sent a messenger into the station to give warning; shortly afterwards, he heard that raids had actually been made in various parts of the district, about the middle of January. These raids were as follows.

The manager of the tea-garden at Monierkhal, had received warning of a raid, and had removed his coolies ; but he with the guard of thirty-seven soldiers and police, and two other Europeans, remained in the stockade. They were reinforced by Mr. Daly, a police-officer, from Cachar, and about forty soldiers.

The Lushais, under Lalboora, however, besieged the stockade for two days, keeping up a very heavy fire. Mr. Daly twice made sorties, but each time was driven back with loss : the Lushais rushing on the slain and plundering their bodies. The Lushais are supposed to have lost fifty men during this attack.

At the same time Lalboora's cousin, Tangdong, had made an attempt to reach Nowarbund, but losing his way came out on the

Nudigram road, where they fell in with a
guard of eight soldiers and a constable. The
Sepoys behaved gallantly, but were overpowered,
six being killed, and one wounded. They are said
to have killed twenty-five of the enemy before being
overcome. Tangdong, on his return to his village,
found that it had been attacked in his absence and
destroyed by a large party of Soktés under Kamhow, and his wife and a large number of his people carried off as captives. In these two affairs
the Lushais got possession of thirteen muskets
from the dead police and Sepoys, which caused
them great exultation.

In South Hylakandy attacks had also been
made on the gardens of Alexandrapur, Jhalua
Chura, and Cantley Chura, by the Howlongs
from the South, assisted by the Lyloos. At
Alexandrapur, early in the morning, the Lushais
emerged suddenly on the garden from the surrounding jungle, taking the people so much by
surprise that no attempt at defence could be
made. Mr. Winchester, who, with his daughter,
was on a visit to a friend at this garden, and
some coolies, were killed at once, the manager

of the garden effecting his escape, and little Mary Winchester and several others being carried off as prisoners.

At the other gardens they were not so successful, the occupants having time to arm themselves before the Lushais appeared, and the latter were repulsed with ease in each attack, and forced to retire altogether. It was against these Howlongs and Lyloos that the operations of the right column, under General Brownlow, were directed, and from whom they succeeded eventually in obtaining the release of Mary Winchester.

While returning from Lushai land Mr. Edgar received a visit from Khalkom, Sukpilal's son, who promised to assist us if an Expedition was undertaken against the Eastern Lushais, and stated that a path from Tipai Mukh, which might be made passable for elephants, led directly into their country.

Mr. Edgar recommended that, if an expedition was sent against Lalboora, Tipai Mukh should be adopted as the starting point, being nearer that chief's villages than any other place accessible by water.

CHAPTER III.

———

EXPEDITION OF 1871—COLONEL RABAN'S RECOMMENDATIONS—
GENERAL BOURCHIER—THE ROUTE—RELATIONS WITH THE
RAJAH OF MUNIPUR—BURMESE INVASIONS—VICISSITUDES
OF MUNIPUR—MAJOR-GENERAL NUTHALL—INROADS OF
THE EASTERN LUSHAI CHIEFS.

CHAPTER III.

IN July, 1871, the Governor-General in Council decided on sending an Expedition against the Lushais. The force was to consist of two columns, one starting from Chittagong, the other from Cachar; a contingent force was also to be supplied by the Rajah of Munipur.

Remembering the former unsuccess of small expeditions which had started late in the season, with badly organized commissariat arrangements, Lord Napier of Magdala, not however without opposition, succeeded in inducing the Government to sanction a much more costly enterprise.

Colonel Raban, who commanded an expedition

from the Chittagong side, in 1861, had, in
giving the results of the experience he then
gained, recommended that in any future operations not less than from twelve to fifteen
hundred fighting men should be sent from that
side; that they should be ready to start from
some point on the Kassalong river, not later
than the first week in December, " and that a
Commissariat officer of some experience, with
an efficient establishment, should be at Chittagong early in November, to make the necessary
arrangements for boats for the conveyance of
troops, &c. The supplies of a less perishable
nature should also be sent on and stored, as
soon as a force sufficient for their protection had
arrived."

He stated that a thousand coolies would
be the smallest number required, and that
Hillmen alone would be of any use; he was
also of opinion that another, though perhaps a
smaller force, should operate at the same time
from the direction of Cachar.

It will be remembered that Colonel Lister
had considered, as early as 1850, that

the smallest force which would make an
impression on the country, would be three
thousand men. In the face of all these recommendations, petty expeditions had been set
on foot late in the season, at various times, with
what miserable results we have already
seen.

In 1871, all the recommendations made by
Colonel Raban ten years before, were carried
out. It was determined that each column
should consist of three regiments, accompanied
by a half-battery of artillery and a company
of Sappers and Miners, representing a force
of nearly two thousand men, with about an
equal number of coolies, and a certain number
of elephants. The detail of the regiments,
&c., which composed the left column, will
be found further on, when we begin to relate
the movements of the column.

Brigadier-General Bourchier, C.B., commanding the North-eastern Frontier District, was
selected to command the Cachar column, and
after a consultation with Mr. Edgar, who
went up to Shillong to give him all the in-

formation he could about the country and routes to it, the General decided that the Tipai Mukh route would be the best, as he had determined to attack Lalboora.

No special instructions had been issued by Government as to the tribes to be punished by the left column, but the reasons which influenced the General and Mr. Edgar to direct their energies against Vonolel's people were the following.

These people had, in 1869 and 1871, been concerned in the raids in Cachar, during which they had obtained great advantages over our Sepoys. They were also the remotest and least accessible of all the Lushais from the Cachar side, and it seemed unlikely "that they, secure in their distant fastnesses, and confident that they were more than a match for our troops in jungle fighting, would be induced to make a voluntary submission by the terror inspired by our punishment of nearer and less warlike tribes than our own." Mr. Edgar also says :—

" General Bourchier considered, and I fully

agreed with him, that the only way in which
we could force these people to submit, and to
recognise that they must behave properly in
future, was to show them that we could reach
them, and that we had the power of crushing
any opposition they could make to our occupation of their country."

As reference has been made to the Rajah
of Munipur several times, and his contingent
was destined to play a certain part in the
Expedition, a glance at our relations with
him may not be considered out of place.

As early as the middle of the eighteenth
century the Munipuris applied to the British
Government for aid against the Burmese,
offering to pay a large annual tribute. It
was determined to assist them, and an officer
with a detachment was sent to their aid. He
was recalled, however, when he had reached
the capital of Cachar; and no further intercourse took place till the first war between
the British and Burmese occurred in 1823.

The Burmese troops invaded Assam and
Cachar, causing great alarm in our frontier

district of Sylhet. Three of the Munipuri
princes who had been quarrelling among themselves, uniting against the common enemy,
begged the protection of the British. Negotiations were opened with them, and a party
of five hundred taken into British pay under
the command of one of these princes, Gumbeer
Sing. With this party, and the assistance of
some British troops, he succeeded in driving
the Burmese, not only from Cachar, but also
from Munipur.

Subsequently this body, increased to two
thousand men, and placed under the command of a Captain Grant, was called the
Munipur Levy.

Captain Grant compelled the Burmese to
retire, and fixed the Nungthé river as
the eastern boundary of Munipur; but at
the desire of the British Government, and
with a view of pleasing the Burmese, this
boundary was given up, and a more westerly
one, the eastern base of the Yomadong Hills,
substituted for it.

The former was certainly the better boundary,

and by giving it up our Government entailed upon itself a monthly expense of Rs. 500, as compensation to Munipur for alienated territory, "and made it necessary, from the predatory habits of the tribes inhabiting the Yomadong Hills constantly endangering it, to secure the peace of the frontier by retaining at Munipur a Political agent."

Gumbeer Sing, having thus, with our assistance, obtained possession of Munipur, was declared independent. On his death, in 1834, a regency was established under Nur Sing, Chunder Kirtee, Gumbeer's son, being an infant.

In 1835 the British Government determined to discontinue all connection with the Munipur troops. Nur Sing was succeeded by his brother Devindro Sing.

Whilst the latter was preparing to ascend the throne, Chunder Kirtee, who had been living in Cachar, returned with a few followers to obtain the kingdom for himself. He crossed the hills, and being joined by most of the adherents of the two last Rajahs, he soon succeeded in driving Devindro Sing out of the country. He fled to Cachar, whither he was afterwards followed by some princes from Munipur, who had become dissatisfied with Chunder Kirtee, and together they made several attacks on the latter.

They were unsuccessful, "but their frequent attempts to upset the Munipur Government were distressing to the country and prejudicial to British influence." Warnings proving useless to deter these men, and being fearful that a prince from Burmah was about to secure possession of the Munipur throne, our Government declared Chunder Kirtee Sing under its especial protection, and undertook to maintain him in his kingdom. The princes in Cachar disregarded this declaration, and were overcome by some British troops sent against them.

Since then, Chunder Kirtee has reigned in peace; a Political Agent being still retained in Munipur.

For some time, Colonel McCulloch was the Political Agent, and from his intimate knowledge

of the character and modes of thought of the
Kookies, and his great experience in frontier
matters, he was able, through Munipur, to
influence the Eastern Lushais under Vonolel,
whom he induced to come to terms, which were
respected as long as the Colonel continued in
Munipur, and during that time friendly relations seem to have existed between the Lushais
and the Ladoés, and the Kookies inhabiting the
southern portion of Munipur; and the latter
used to shoot over the hunting-grounds of the
Lushais, in the neighbourhood of the salt-springs
of Chiboo.

In the Spring of 1870, however, the Lushais
lost seven men at this place, in an affray with
some Ladoés. Mr. Edgar thought that this,
and the consequent bad feeling which was
generated between the Munipuris and Lushais,
were due principally to the decline of the influence of the Political Agent over the Kookies,
and his inability to control the intrigues of the
Munipur officials; and he considered that the
Rajah himself would be willing to carry out a
friendly policy, as it was manifestly to his ad-

vantage to have in the friendly Lushais a strong barrier between his frontier and the powerful and savage tribes beyond, such as the Soktés and Khyrens. And if the Political Agent had taken up a position with a tolerably strong force at Chiboo in December, 1870, it is probable that the Eastern Lushai chiefs would not have dared to make the raids in January, 1871, which have been already described.

The Rajah of Munipur volunteered to assist the last Expedition with a contingent force of five hundred men, under the command of two Munipur officers; and the Government of India, in accepting his services, directed him to place the contingent under the orders of General Bourchier.

Major-General Nuthall, an officer of great experience on this frontier, was appointed to accompany the Munipur force, as Political Agent; through him the Rajah was requested to establish outposts along the hills east of Tipai Mukh, and south of the Munipur valley, and to advance his force south of Moirang, in the direction of Chiboo, with a view of pro-

tecting the Munipur valley, and while securing
the fidelity of Kamhow and preventing him
from aiding the Lushais, to enable the Munipur
State to take every advantage of his assistance.
At the same time this movement would tend
to prevent the Lushais from retiring towards
the East in our advance from Tipai Mukh,
and afterwards closing on our rear and cutting
off our communications.

CHAPTER IV.

THE TOPOGRAPHICAL SURVEY OF INDIA—COOLIES—CACHAR—
MUNIPUR HORSE-DEALERS — HOCKEY-PLAYERS — UNCOM-
FORTABLE MODE OF RIDING—PRESENT FOR A CHIEF—TEA-
GARDENS—NATIVE IDOLS—THE MONIERKHAL STOCKADE—
RUMOURS OF A THREATENED ATTACK—CURIOUS DISCOVERY.

CHAPTER IV.

IN July, 1871, I was appointed to the Topographical Survey Department of India, and when the Expedition against the Lushais was decided on, I was fortunate enough to be attached to the party under orders to accompany the Left Column, and proceeded to join it in Cachar.

I arrived in Silchar, the principal station of this district, on the 12th November. The party consisted of Captain Badgley in charge, Lieutenant Leach, R.E., three Civil Surveyors, and myself. We had also a large establishment of instrument-carriers, and three sets of instruments.

This large party had been sanctioned on the

recommendation of the Commander-in-Chief, who remembered the good results obtained from the employment of a strong Survey party in Abyssinia.

Very little was known about the disposition of the tribes at that time, and very few expected that any opposition would be offered to the advance of the troops. It was therefore thought that, with the co-operation of Sukpilal, about whose friendliness no doubts were entertained, the Survey would be able to send out detached parties in various directions, or to accompany the troops, should the advance from Tipai Mukh be made by separate columns taking different routes. This, however, did not happen.

The advance, as will be seen, was made by one column in a continuous line, and the Survey had no opportunity of sending out detached parties off the line of march below Tipai Mukh.

We had been informed that coolies would be supplied to us by the Commissariat in Cachar. On applying, however, to the officer in charge of that Department, he showed us his orders, which were to supply us, if possible. These words gave him a loop-hole for escape, and pressed as he was by the mortality among the coolies at Chattuck, he gladly availed himself of it, and we were eventually obliged to procure Cossyah coolies from Shillong.

These men proved as good coolies as any with the Expedition; but the delay consequent on the time spent in securing them, caused us to lose a month of very valuable time.

We found it difficult even to get coolies for short periods to enable us to move about in Cachar; so that instead of accompanying the Quartermaster-General's Department from the outset, and taking advantage of the many checks which occurred before Tipai Mukh was reached by the troops, to clear and fix points on either side of the Barak in Cachar and Munipur, while it was still safe to travel almost without a guard, we were condemned to a state of irritating inaction.

At first Cachar was in a great state of

bustle, the different corps and bodies of coolies
arriving daily. The coolies were of all races,
Punjabis and Hindustanis from up-country,
Mekirs, Nagas, Cachari Kookies from the North
Cachar Hills, and Nepaulese Goorkhas.

All these men, on arrival, were supplied each
with a blanket, coat, boots, a daô, and
bandages for the legs, as protection against
thorns ; and large tarpaulins—in the proportion, I think, of one to every four coolies—were
also distributed to them.

The hospital coolies, for the sake of dis-
tinction, received bandages of bright yellow,
which, contrasting in a very striking manner
with their brown legs and general dinginess,
gave them a sufficiently marked appearance.
We had the pleasure of seeing corps after
corps march in, to be supplied with coolies,
and after obtaining the number apportioned to
each, march out again.

By the end of November we were left to
ourselves, and Silchar had settled down once
more into its usual dead level of dulness.
The Munipur horsedealers, who inhabit villages

near Silchar, and had been doing a brisk trade in selling their active, hardy little ponies to officers going on the Expedition, were left to their general amusement of hockey. Their recommendation of ponies as good hockey-players to men who required them simply as baggage animals, and who were going into almost impenetrable jungles, seemed unnecessary; nevertheless it was one on which they strongly insisted when there appeared to be any hesitation in giving them the price which they demanded.

A very curious sight is presented by the Munipur hockey-ground. The sturdy, active, little ponies enter, to all appearances, into the game as thoroughly as their riders, following the ball with great rapidity, while they wheel and turn in every direction, as if at once responsive to the least emotion of the lithe and naked natives mounted on them. Now the field is scattered. One man is seen riding away in the distance after the ball, which he strikes up towards the goal, when a simultaneous rush is made by all the players towards it, and nothing is seen but a confused mass of ponies' legs and hockey sticks whirling high in air. The ball again gets free, the field scatter in pursuit, and a similar scene is once more enacted.

This game, which is being introduced into England, affords ample opportunity for the display of good riding, and is much patronized by the planters in Cachar, who hold weekly meetings for the practice of it.

Many of the Munipuris ride without stirrups, and those who have them simply cling to them by holding the stirrup-iron between the toes, a most uncomfortable way of riding, according to our ideas. As a protection to the bare legs of the riders when passing through the jungle, they have huge flaps of hard leather suspended from the saddle on each side, descending as low as the stirrups, and turned round in front. These articles, which are anything but ornamental, give a most uncouth appearance to the saddle, and flap about with a tremendous noise when the pony is going at all fast.

While we were in Cachar, presents arrived at the Deputy-Commissioner's for Sukpilal. They consisted of a large silver-gilt goblet and claret jug, with inscriptions to the effect that they were presented by the Government of India in recognition of his former services.

It is sad to think that these not very appropriate ornaments for a rough bamboo house, where they would have shone conspicuously on the floor from among the family stock of yams, potatoes, &c., never found their way to Sukpilal at all, though they accompanied Mr. Edgar through the Expedition. The chief, fo whom they were intended, had conducted himself in so unsatisfactory a manner that it was not considered proper to present them to him, and they returned to Cachar. They might have been presented to some other deserving chief, but the English inscription engraved on them rendered them unfit for such a purpose.

Our coolies arrived at last from Shillong on the 14th December, and that same evening Captain Badgley received a telegram from the

General, directing him to send a survey officer
at once to join the head-quarters, as orders had
been sent by the Government to the commanders
of each column, to communicate daily by
telegraph to each other, through the Commander-
in-Chief's office. They were directed to give
the latitude and longitude of each camp, with
any other information likely to facilitate the
junction of the two columns, should this be
found possible before the close of the Expedition.

Captain Badgley himself left the next day
to join the head-quarters, leaving the remainder
of the party to follow by two routes, one by
Luckipur and the Barak, the other by the
Buban Range to Mynadhur.

The latter route fell to me. With one of
our civil surveyors, Mr. Ogle, I left Silchar on
the 16th of December, and marched out as far
as a tea-garden called Borvalia, about eighteen
miles along a level road.

Here we were very hospitably received and
entertained by the manager, Mr. Willington, and
his wife, who also found accommodation for our
classis and coolies.

The next morning, lightly equipped, we started to ascend to a point on the range which had been cleared, and from which we expected to get some work. This point, though apparently an easy day's journey from the bungalow, proved very difficult to reach. The path, a very obscure one, is used by the garden coolies and others who go occasionally to worship a stone god and goddess whose shrine is near the place towards which we were proceeding.

Mr. Willington gave us two coolies as guides, without whose assistance we should never have discovered the way, which for the first three miles lay through very tall and tangled grass jungle, of so rough and hard a texture that our faces and hands were cut by it as if by knives. The path was sometimes lost in swamps, but again appearing, followed the course of small streams alive with innumerable leeches, which fastened on us without the slightest provocation.

At last, after crossing a series of low hills and spurs, we reached the foot of the Bubans.

Here, crossing a beautiful stream of clear water, the ascent commenced, and a stiff climb it proved; a sheer ascent of eighteen hundred feet, with a slope of three hundred and thirty-two feet the whole way. Arrived at the top, we had a long five miles to go over a very uneven path, ascending and descending alternately, never level.

Darkness closed around us long before we reached our camping ground; but lighting candles, we distributed them among the coolies at intervals, and managed, though slowly and with difficulty, to find the spot—a very romantic little place, enclosed on three sides by huge masses of fern and moss-covered rocks, the fourth sloping steeply down to a little spring of good water.

, Beneath these rocks we found the rudely carved figures of the god and goddess, about three feet high, with strips of red and white cloth adorning their shapeless bodies. The former was sitting cross-legged on some broken stones, on which were some attempts at ornamentation, and which were apparently the remains of a kind of canopy, or at any rate, of a throne. The goddess was standing in a small low-walled enclosure, and at the foot of a bamboo bedstead, which had been erected by some visitors from the garden a few days before.

. Having lighted a fire, and killed, cooked, and eaten a fowl, we made our beds, and were speedily asleep under the shelter of the goddess near whose shrine we were lying, though to acknowledge the truth, she was a somewhat fear-inspiring object, as seen dimly through the musquito curtains by the pale moonlight, to a nervous imagination in moments of half-wakefulness.

I was unable to find out anything about these figures, how long they had been there, whom they represented, &c. The men with us did not seem to know anything about them, though they prostrated themselves with great reverence before them.

The next morning, having done what we could from this point, which commands a most extensive view of North Cachar and Munipur, we returned, camping at the foot of the hills for the night, and proceeding early next day to Mr. Willington's to breakfast, and pick up the men and instruments we had left behind at the gardens.

Here I must express my sense of obligation to all the planters whose gardens we visited, for the great hospitality they invariably showed us. The fact that we were strangers, and in need of any sort of assistance, was a sufficient passport to their liberality, and we were indebted to them for much valuable help in many ways.

In the afternoon we went to Sonai Mukh, whence we proceeded the next day to Monierkhal. The road running along the Sonai is very level as far as Nagakhal, a stream at the foot of the hills three miles beyond Monierkhal. It at first runs through very flat open country, but below Nudigram it passes through a large patch of very high grass jungle, beyond which it enters a forest, and so to Nagakhal, passing two clearances for gardens, Durmiakhal and Monierkhal.

The latter, now famous by reason of the

frequent raids made upon it, is a tolerably large clearance. The dark green tea-plants, growing on the low hills or tilas, give a curious speckled appearance to the sandy mounds; on one of which stands the stockade, containing small barracks and a magazine. Just beneath are the coolie huts, and the small stockade beyond them, which commands the bridge over the Sonai, and the opening in the belt of forest surrounding the garden whence the Lushais generally emerge.

The Monierkhal stockade, as well as that at Mynadhur, is not nearly so remarkable for engineering skill as any of the Lushai defences we came across. The bungalow is situated on a small tila about two hundred yards north of the stockade.

On arriving at Monierkhal we found the Moniejer was absent, and the garden Baboo, the guard, and every one else, in a great state of excitement, as a notice had been sent from Mynadhur that a hundred Lushais were supposed to be going in the Monierkhal direction. Everything had been moved out of

F

the bungalow into the stockade, whither also the coolies' wives and children had been sent for safety, and an attack was confidently expected.

Early next morning, while the mists were still hanging over the garden, the head Baboo, evidently an inventive genius, informed us on the authority of a friend supposed to be at Tipai Mukh, whom, however, I suspected to be a Bengali Mrs. Harris, that the General had been defeated in a great fight with the Lushais, and was retreating to Tipai Mukh, as fast as the elephants, by which the line of march was much encumbered, would let him. All this sounded very circumstantial, but we told the Baboo we would not put much faith in his friend's statement.

The night and morning passed off without anything occurring to disturb our peaceful slumbers, and about 9 A.M. we commenced the journey to Mynadhur, across the Bubans.

On the highest point of the mountains we found, to our surprise, a large native bedstead by the path, and afterwards heard that it be-

longed to some luxurious commissariat or post-
office Baboo, who had managed to get it so
far, when the coolie, who was carrying it,
refused to take it any further and abandoned
it. It now serves as a convenient resting
place on which the weary travellers may re-
cline after their fatiguing climb, and from
which they may survey the smiling plains of
Cachar spread out like a map some three
thousand feet below.

The stillness of the forest was ever and
anon broken by the cries of a black monkey,
known among the natives as the " hoolook."
These animals go about in troops, uttering
cries very much resembling the yelping of
beaten puppies. One or two commence with
a few single cries in one key, when suddenly
the whole pack join the chorus in every variety
of key. After indulging in this amusement for
some time, it is brought to a close, the cries
gradually dying away, but only to be resumed
again with greater vigour than before. We
seldom saw these monkeys, but we heard them
frequently as far down as Kungnung.

Mynadhur, which is elsewhere described, was reached about half-past six in the afternoon, and here we had our first experience of Commissariat rations. I went into the little hut and saw, on the ground, two dark masses covered with the prevailing sand, and, on investigation, I found they were my beef and pork for a week.

I need not repeat my remarks about the road between Mynadhur and Tipai Mukh. Suffice it to say that, journeying by land and water, we reached the latter place just in time for dinner on Christmas Day.

Difficulties connected with the Commissariat Department prevented our going on to the front till the 2nd of January, when we started for Tuibum. On the road we met all the wounded from the Kholel business, whom they were taking into the dépôt hospital at Tipai Mukh. We reached No. 7 Station on the 4th.

CHAPTER V.

THE LUSHAIS—CHARACTERISTICS OF THREE PRINCIPAL TRIBES
—FEATURES AND COMPLEXION—MUSCULAR STRENGTH—IN-
TELLECTUAL APTITUDE—COSTUME—PERSONAL ADORNMENT—
A LUSHAI EXQUISITE — PRACTICE OF SMOKING — TOBACCO
WATER—WEAPONS—GUNPOWDER.

CHAPTER V.

THE Lushais with whom we became ac-
quainted during our journeyings, belonged to
three different tribes, the Lushais, Paités,' or
Soktés, and Pois. The latter are rather taller
and of a fairer complexion than the ordinary
run of Hillmen, but the principal distinguish-
ing characteristic between the three tribes is
the mode in which they dress their hair.

The Lushai parts his hair in the middle,
and braiding it smoothly on each side of the
face, binds it in a knot on the nape of the
neck, secured by large copper or steel hair-
pins; the Sokté does not part it at all, but
wears it short and standing out like flames
round the forehead, which is generally rather

high and round; sometimes the hair is twisted into a little tail at the back.

The Pois part their hair across the back of the head, from ear to ear, all above this line being drawn upwards or forwards, bound in a high double knot on the forehead, and fastened by a small ivory or bone comb, generally ornamented with some little design in red; but all the hair below the parting is allowed to hang in wavy curls over the back and shoulders.

Some Pois, once in camp, were watching a Sikh Sepoy performing his toilet, and seeing that, previous to putting on his turban, he bound his long hair into a knot on the top of his head, tying one end of the turban into it, they at once hailed him as a Poi and a brother. Bearing in mind these distinctions, the following description applies to all, premising that the only women we saw were Lushais.

Both the men and women are well made, and very muscular; the average height of the former appeared to be about five feet six inches, and of the women, five feet four inches. The men are all sturdy fellows, thickset as to the

neck and shoulders, body light and active,
arms and legs muscular and well developed,
their arms generally long in proportion to their
bodies.

Their complexion comprises every shade of
brown, and their features vary considerably;
the generality however possessing flat retroussé
noses with wide nostrils, thick lips, and
small almond-shaped eyes. Among the Lushais
though, and especially among those related to
the reigning families, some of whom were
even handsome, we met with a much more
refined type—the nose being thin and aquiline
with small nostrils, the lips thin and the
mouth small. In all, however, the cheek-bones
were high and prominent, the face broad and
remarkable for an almost entire absence of
beard or moustache; even a slight moustache
and small tuft of hair on the chin being the
exception rather than the rule.

The expression of many was bright and intelligent, and they showed a wonderful aptitude
for quickly understanding anything new and
wonderful which they saw during their visits

to our camp. Not the least astonishing proof
of this was the sharpness they displayed in
understanding at a glance the intention of a
pencil sketch. I showed a sketch to some
Lushais one day, and it pleased them so much
that one went away and returned with the
skulls of a deer and a pig, and a live hen,
all of which he requested me to draw, which
I did; and the lookers-on pointed out, on the
models, each part as it was delineated, even to
some discolorations on the skulls, which I indicated by a little shading.

Their general expression of wonder is " Amakeh
oh !" which they repeat to each other over
and over again, when anything more astonishing than usual excites their interest. Their
dress consists only of one large homespun
sheet of cotton cloth, passed round the
body under the right arm, which is thus
left free, the two ends being thrown in opposite directions over the left shoulder, where
they are secured by a strap of tiger or otter
skin, supporting a bag in which is carried a
knife, a dâo, tobacco, flint, steel, and other
little necessaries.

The articles contained in the bag are protected from the rain by a kind of shield made of tiger, bear, or goat-skin; the latter, with the long hair pendent, strongly resembling a Highland sporan. This shield is fastened at each end of the strap, and can be easily removed at will. The cloth is generally greyish white, with a dark blue stripe running through it; but sometimes it is dark blue, with a few stripes of white, yellow, or red, or all three interwoven into it.

Occasionally we met a young man, apparently a Lushai Exquisite, who wore both the white and blue cloths arranged with no little taste.

A few tartans have found their way among the Lushais, but these have been procured through Munipur or Cachar. The men wear necklaces of coloured beads, or of amber, which are worn, in large cylindrical beads. We saw very few of the latter and those only on people apparently of some importance.

A large tiger's tooth mounted in silver, and suspended round the neck by a thread, is much prized, and has, I believe, some special virtue as a charm. A large red stone, suspended by a string, often forms an ornament for the ear, but a bunch of small brilliant feathers, or a small tuft of goat's hair, dyed crimson or blue, and passed through a hole in the lobe of the ear, seemed to be the favourite ornament of that organ. Muntries and certain other head-men are allowed to wear a tuft of feathers in the knots of their hair.

The women we saw seemed to disdain these ornaments, but some of them distended the lobes of their ears by a small thick circular disc of white baked clay. They wear a small strip of cloth, eighteen inches deep, passed round the waist, and over this, a cloth of dark blue wrapped carefully about them, in which they carry their young children on their backs.

Their mode of dressing their hair is exceedingly pretty; it is braided smoothly over the forehead and plaited at the sides, the plaits being passed round the back of the head and over the top in the manner of a coronet.

Men, women, and children, from the age at

which they can hold a pipe, smoke almost in-
cessantly. The mens' pipes are made sometimes
of brass, rudely ornamented, but generally of a
small piece of bamboo lined with copper or iron;
a very fine bamboo being let in near the knot as
a mouthpiece.

The bowl of the women's pipe is of clay, and
is fitted with a bamboo receptacle for water,
which, becoming impregnated with the fumes of
the smoke and the oil of the tobacco, is afterwards
carried about by the men in small gourds or
bamboo tubes, and sipped from time to time,
being kept in the mouth for a short time before
spitting it out. This tobacco water is looked
upon as a great luxury, and when a Lushai meets
a friend, he offers it to him as a mark of
courtesy, as civilized old gentlemen used formerly
to exchange snuff-boxes.

The Lushais are mighty hunters, as they are
great eaters of flesh, and their supplies depend
a good deal upon the success of their hunting
excursions. It is only within the last fifteen years,
or thereabouts, that they have learnt the use of
fire-arms, but now they possess a large number of

muskets, most of which are old flint-locks, of
English manufacture, bearing the Tower mark of
various dates, some as far back as the middle of
the last century. The stocks of these are highly
varnished and ornamented with red paint.

Their other arms are bows made of bamboo,
with which poisoned arrows are used. These,
however, I believe, are not much used now, having
given way to the superior claims of powder and
shot. Spears of various shapes and lengths,
they obtain from Munipur, Cachar, and elsewhere. The dâo is a triangular blade of about
twelve inches long, fitted into a wooden handle.
The edge is sharpened for cutting, and the broad
end is employed for digging. This, besides being
used as a weapon of offence, is also the agricultural implement with which most of their
jooming operations are performed.

A long-bladed two-handed Burmese knife, slung
over the shoulder, is carried by some with an
air of superiority. Small bamboo quivers, full of
panjies, *i.e.*, small pointed stakes of hardened
bamboo, are in time of war attached to their bags.
These are stuck in the ground along the path in

escaping from a pursuer, or in the approach to a village, and are capable of inflicting very nasty wounds in bare feet, and will even penetrate thick leather shoes.

Formerly the Lushais used to obtain gunpowder from Cachar and Chittagong. Owing to the increased vigilance of the authorities in these districts, they are now obliged to manufacture it for themselves. Sulphur they get from Burmah; the saltpetre they obtain from heaps of manure collected in large funnel-shaped baskets which hang up outside the houses. This manure is strongly impregnated with urine, and the liquid, draining through into receptacles beneath, is afterwards evaporated, and crystals of saltpetre are obtained.

Their powder is very weak, but what is lacking in quality they make up in quantity, about four fingers, or six drachms, being the usual charge. The bullets are generally bits of iron or lead hammered into shape.

Their powder-flasks are made from metua horns, polished and ornamented with little bands of red cane-work, and sometimes inlaid with silver; the priming powder is carried in a very small horn.

CHAPTER VI.

LUSHAI VILLAGES—CONSTRUCTION OF THE HOUSES—INTERNAL
ARRANGEMENTS — WINDOWS — STOCKADES—NATIVE WINE —
BASKET-MAKING — DOMESTIC ANIMALS — CURIOUS MACHINE
FOR ENTRAPPING GAME — AGRICULTURAL OPERATIONS —
MUSICAL INSTRUMENTS—A SMITH'S FORGE.

G

CHAPTER VI.

A LUSHAI village is generally situated on or
near the top of some high hill or ridge.
Those we saw were seldom built on the highest
part, but a little way down the slope, apparently
for protection against high winds. The houses
are constructed on one uniform plan; they are
all gable-ended and raised some three or four
feet from the ground. The framework is of
timber, very strong, the walls and floor being of
bamboo matting, and the roof thatched with grass,
or with a palmated leaf common in the hills.

The houses are usually about eighteen feet long
by twelve wide, and in front is a large verandah,
fitted with hollow basins scooped out of tree
trunks, in which rice is husked with long wooden
pestles.

At the back of the house is another small enclosed verandah, which serves as a sort of store-
room. The interior of the house is fitted with a
large hearth of mud or flat stones, over which is
suspended a large square wooden framework, on
which are trays of grain, herbs, &c., all dried,
bacon cured, &c.

On one side of the fire-place is a small raised
sleeping place.

The doors are blocked up at the bottom
with small logs, for a height of about two
feet. This, I was told, was with a view to
keep the small children in, and the pigs out.
A small circular hole affords entrance to the
domestic fowls; and small cages constructed just
under the eaves are the abode of fowls and
pigeons at night. The door itself is a close
bamboo hurdle, sliding backwards and forwards
inside on a couple of bamboos, which act as guides.

Some houses have windows, which are closed
externally by shutters of a similar construction to
the doors. The front of the house is covered with
skulls of antlered deer, metua, bears, leopards,
&c., all smoked to a dark brown colour. Feathers

of various birds are also stuck into the interstices of the wall.

The chief's house is of similar construction, but much larger, being about forty yards long, by ten wide, and is divided within into one large hall, and two or three sleeping rooms opening on to a passage running the whole length of the building. It has, generally, in front a large level open space, and from this the streets radiate in all directions, following the spurs or slopes of the hill. The whole is inclosed in a stiff timber stockade, excellently constructed on the most approved principle, with a ditch and banquettes in rear and loopholed. The entrance is through a passage of strong timbers, and defended by a thick door or gates.

Small, well-protected look-outs are erected at the angles of the stockade, commanding the approaches to the village. Outside the fencing, timber platforms surrounded by posts, each crowned with the skull of some animal, mark the spot "where the rude forefathers of the hamlet sleep." Inside also, these resting places are marked by a small raised mound of earth, or a pile of stones and a few skulls, usually close to the house of the deceased.

Outside every house is a small raised platform, on which, and on the stones covering the graves of their deceased friends, the Lushais assemble in groups in the mornings and evenings to smoke and converse.

In all the villages, moreover, there is a large barn-like building, raised similarly to the houses, but partially open at the sides, and with a square sunk fireplace in the middle. This is the house of assembly, where the affairs of the village and the arrangements for raiding expeditions, &c., are discussed.

The Lushais manufacture a kind of wine from fermented rice and water; something else is added, a fruit, found in the jungle, I believe, but what it was, I could not find out. These ingredients are placed in a large clay jar, and pressed down for several days, when the wine is fit to drink. In one of the northern villages we saw them sucking the wine out of the jar, by means of a long reed, which was passed from mouth to mouth; but further south we found in the houses a kind of syphon, made by joining a couple of reeds together at an angle of forty-five degrees, by means of a piece of India-rubber. This is used for drawing off the wine from the rice, &c., in the jar. The wine is thin, and in flavour somewhat resembles cranberry wine.

The Lushais are very clever at basket-work, making baskets of all sorts, of cane or bamboo, from little really tasteful ones for holding small articles in-doors, up to large deep baskets with conical lids, and little feet, in which they carry loads of all sorts. The latter are carried on the back, a small cane-band passing round them, and through the ends of a little wooden yoke on the shoulders, and so over the forehead.

The domestic animals found in a Lushai village are the metua, a very handsome animal of the bovine race, with fine horns; the goat, remarkable for his very long white hair; pigs, which are fattened up to a great size, and fowls. We saw a few dogs in some of the villages we occupied.

Near the villages we found various kinds of traps, some formed by bending down a strong sapling or bamboo as a spring, which jerks

the animal high into the air, holding it suspended by one foot. A sepoy with the right
column was caught in one of these, and carried
suddenly aloft by the foot, to the astonishment
of his comrades.

Another trap, for tigers, &c., is a rough cage
of logs, open at both ends, the top of which is
composed of several large trunks of trees so
arranged as to fall on and crush any animal
passing through the cage. They are also very
skilful in making small rat-traps and snares for
birds.

A Lushai field, or joom, as it is called, is
merely a piece of ground on the hill-side,
cleared of jungle in the following manner. A
convenient piece of ground having been fixed
upon, the undergrowth of shrubs and creepers
is cut, and all except the largest trees felled;
the fallen jungle is then left to dry in the
sun, so that it may be fired when the proper
season arrives.

Great caution is exercised in firing the jooms,
to prevent the flames spreading, as at this
season of the year the surrounding jungle is

very dry. When the joom is fired, all the felled jungle, with the exception of the larger trees, is reduced to ashes; the unburnt trees are left lying on the ground, and help to keep the soil from being washed down by rain. The soil also is thoroughly burnt for an inch or two, and this soil, being mixed with the ashes, becomes fit for the reception of the seed.

Baskets of mixed seeds of cotton, rice, melons, pumpkins, yams, &c., are carried by the sowers, and a handful thrown into little narrow holes made with the broad end of a daô.

The sowing takes place just before the rains, during which the villagers assist each other in weeding the crops.

The first thing to ripen is Indian corn, in the end of July; afterwards, in order, melons and vegetables; lastly rice and other grain in September. Small houses, six or eight feet from the ground, are erected in the jooms, and are occupied, during the ripening of the crops, by men whose business it is to keep off monkeys, jungle-fowl, &c., who would do mischief in the jooms.

The rice, having been cut and beaten out,

is stored in granaries fenced about with strong logs. Like the people of "Hammelin town," the Lushais are frequently visited by immense numbers of rats which overrun everything, filling the granaries, and leaving ruin and devastation behind them. "Neither fire nor water stops the progress of the innumerable host, which disappear as suddenly and mysteriously as they arrive."

Besides the crops grown in the fields, small gardens are frequent in the villages, in which are cultivated yams, tobacco, pepper, beans of various sorts, and herbs. In carrying loads or cutting jungle, the Lushais work to the cry of a continuous "haw-haw" uttered in measured time by all.

Their musical instruments are few and simple; a drum of stretched deer-skin, a curious instrument formed from a gourd, the neck of which is furnished with a reed mouth-piece. Into the gourd, seven reed-pipes of various lengths, each having one hole stop, are inserted; the junctions of the reeds with the gourd being rendered air-tight by a stopping of India-rubber. The simple music produced is that of a few notes of a harmonium played low and softly. Another instrument is a single reed-pipe, and they have gongs of various sizes.

The men and boys whistle through their fingers with great power. The songs of the Lushais are low monotonous chants, accompanied by the gourd instrument or drum.

As a rule, a Lushai village is a long distance from any great supply of water; in consequence the Lushais bathe but seldom, and they are unable to manage a boat, or swim. They seem to have few diseases, and only one man did we see marked with small-pox.

Besides manufacturing cotton cloth, making baskets, &c., they work a little in iron. A rough but ingenious forge is found in all their villages. It is similar to one in use all over Lower Bengal, and they have probably learned its construction and use from the Bengali captives.

The forge consists of a couple of wooden cylinders about two feet high, and eight or nine inches in diameter, each furnished with wooden pistons, feathers being fastened to the circumference of the latter as a stuffing to prevent the escape of air. The cylinders are placed upright in the ground, being buried to a certain depth.

A small fire-place of stones is constructed in front, and two thin bamboos communicate under-ground between this and the cylinders. The forge is worked by a man holding the pistons, one in each hand, and moving them alternately, thus keeping up a constant supply of air. The fuel used is charcoal.

A very useful spoon, which serves a variety of purposes, is made from bamboo. A portion about a foot long is cut off above a joint, and the bamboo afterwards cut, as in making a quill pen; a scoop with a long handle is made in two minutes.

The bamboo has rightly been called the Hillman's friend, because it supplies him with everything from a house down to a small drinking-cup. I have referred in the course of this chapter to many of the various uses to which it is put, but there is one which I have not mentioned, its use as a vessel in which to carry water from the stream. The women perform this operation, each carrying about half-a-dozen long and large bamboos on her back, supported in the manner already described.

Our march through the country not being a peaceful one, we had no opportunity of witnessing any of their religious, marriage, or funeral ceremonies, and as in several particulars I find that the Lushais on our side differ from those described by Captain Lewin as dwelling on the Chittagong side, approaching more nearly the descriptions given by Major McCulloch of the Kookies dwelling in the South of Munipur, any quotations made from these authorities might be liable to the charge of inaccuracy, when applied to the tribes with whom we were brought in contact.

With a few exceptions the Lushais impressed us very favourably. Intelligent, merry, and with few wants, they were very far removed from the utterly irreclaimable savages which, prior to the Expedition, our fancy had painted.

CHAPTER VII.

—◦◦◦—

LEFT COLUMN OF THE EXPEDITION—THE COMMISSARIAT DE-
PARTMENT—POLITICAL OFFICER—SILCHAR—THE ARTILLERY
AND SAPPERS—FIRST CASUALTY OF THE CAMPAIGN—ROUTE
FROM SILCHAR TO MYNADHUE — APPEARANCE OF THE
COUNTRY—DIFFICULTIES OF THE MARCH.

CHAPTER VII.

THE Cachar or left column of the Lushai Expedition consisted of the following troops :— Half of the Peshawur mountain battery of artillery under Captain Blackwood, R.A.; one company of Sappers and Miners under Lieutenant Harvey, R.E.; five hundred men of the Punjaub Native Infantry under Colonel Stafford : the same number of the 42nd Assam Light Infantry under Colonel Rattray, C.B.; the same number of the 44th Assam Light Infantry under Colonel Hicks; and one hundred police under Mr. Daly.

Lieutenant-Colonel Davidson, who was in charge of the Commissariat Department, had one thousand two hundred coolies, and several elephants, placed under his orders. A coolie corps consist-

H

ing of eight hundred men intended for the carriage of the Sepoys' baggage, was enrolled under Major Moore and Captain Branson, assisted by Captain Hedayat, native aide-de-camp to the Commander-in-Chief.*

The conduct of the operations of the left column was entrusted to Brigadier-General Bourchier, C.B., commanding the North-eastern Frontier district. On his Staff were Lieutenant-Colonel F. Roberts, R.A., V.C., C.B., Deputy-Assist.-Quartermaster-General, Capt. H. Thompson, Brigade Major; and Captain Butler, Aide-de-Camp. Dr. Buckle, Inspector-General of Hospitals, was in medical charge, and Mr. Edgar Deputy-Commissioner of Cachar, accompanied the column as Political Officer.

A gentleman named Burland, of great experience on this frontier, who had visited the Lushais with Mr. Edgar previously, was appointed to act as Assistant Political Officer. His health, however, failed, and he never got beyond No. 7

---

* A party from the telegraph department, under Mr. Pitman, and one of the Topographical Survey, under Captain Badgley, were also attached to this column.

Camp, and had to relinquish his appointment long before the return of the Expedition.

Silchar, the Sudder, *i.e.*, principal station of the Cachar District, is a small place boasting only of a few brick buildings, including the cutcherry or court-house, and church.

There is a large native bazaar, the houses in which, as well as those of most of the European residents, are built of bamboo and mud. There are two large European shops, which, taking advantage of the necessities of the troops that composed the Expedition, raised their prices enormously. They had no fixed scale, but the price of their goods was raised when the demand for them became much greater than usual. An article which could be obtained on our arrival at Cachar for one rupee, commanded four rupees during the fortnight or so in which the place was occupied by our troops.

It is a very quiet little station, and such an exciting event as the passing through of so many troops, lifted it entirely out of its normal state of level dulness; and " Let us make hay while the sun shines," was apparently the motto adopted

by all classes of shop-keepers, European as well
as native.

This being the nearest station to Tipai Mukh,
it was fixed upon as the rendezvous of the various
corps comprising the Force, and thither all their
special equipments, waterproof sheets, boots, tools,
Norton's pumps, &c., had been sent on by water.
The different corps which arrived in Silchar came
from Abbdabad, Roorkee, and Assam.

The Artillery and Sappers were conveyed from
Calcutta in a Government steamer as far as
Chattuck, on the River Soorma, picking up the
22nd P. N. on their way at Dacca.

A camp was formed at a place called Kala
Rokka a few miles above Chattuck, above which
the state of the river prevented any steamer proceeding. From this place, as soon as country
boats could be obtained, they were brought into
Cachar.

The first casualty of the campaign occurred
on board the Government steamer. It suddenly
grounded, and a flat attached to it, missing the
shoal, went ahead, snapping the hawsers. One
of these flying back, caught a native attached to

the battery, and broke his leg so badly that immediate amputation was necessary.

The 44th arrived from Shillong on the 9th November, the Artillery and Sappers on the 18th; and the 22nd and 42nd a few days later.

The General and Staff had arrived about the 16th, and the next few days were devoted to the distribution of the waterproof sheets, boots, &c., to the troops and coolies; and to the reduction of the kits of officers and men to the appointed limits of weight, twenty seers, or about forty pounds for an officer, and twelve for a sepoy. Each corps was also supplied with coolies and inspected by the General.

While the General was in Silchar, he saw reasons for coming to the conclusion that the posts already established on the Sylhet and Cachar frontier were not sufficiently far south, either to protect his right flank, or to enable him to bring any pressure upon Sukpilal and Khalkom, should they throw in their lot with the Howlongs, or Eastern tribes, and therefore, ordered the officer commanding the 4th N.I., then stationed in Cachar, to occupy a hill called

Benkong on the Noonvai range, and another point on the Rengtipahar, near the Koloshib Hill, cutting roads from them to the Sonai and Dullesur rivers respectively, in order to bring these posts into communication by water with Cachar—arrangements which were most successfully carried out.

General Nuthall had been requested to move the Rajah of Munipur to post detachments on the Southern frontier, flanked by a force near the Nivirang Lake. So great, however, were the difficulties which interfered with the accomplishment of this design, that these posts were never established.

Great doubt had existed as to the best route from Silchar to Mynadhur. Two routes were possible; one over the Buban range *viâ* Monierkhal; and the other round by Luckipur and the banks of the Barak.

The former was the one originally intended to be adopted. The road for three miles beyond Monierkhal was nearly level, but from thence the existing path led up the face of the hill, certainly at a very steep gradient, crossing the range at nearly its highest point.

Colonel Roberts, and Colonel Nuthall of the 44th N.I., went out to explore this route; but, unaccustomed as they then were to hill-climbing and steep rough paths, the difficulties which presented themselves seemed to them insurmountable. They failed, moreover, to find water anywhere between the foot of the range on the one side, and Mynadhur on the other, and consequently all idea of adopting this route was abandoned.

The next thing to be done was to find the path which, though seldom used, was said to exist between Luckipur and Mynadhur, and accordingly some Cachari Kookies were sent out to look for it.

The whole of the country on either bank of the Barak is very difficult. Long spurs are sent down from the Bubans on one side, and the Noonjaibong range on the other. These run steeply down to the very water's edge, and are separated from each other by deep and boggy ravines, and covered with the densest jungle.

The coolies, having either found some elephants' tracks, or observed paths used by wood-

cutters, or, which is more likely, having cut
one out for themselves straight ahead, shirking
no obstacles, returned to report their success,
and the 44th were sent out to improve and widen
the path so discovered, and make it practicable
for laden elephants — a portion of the pro-
gramme which was never accomplished.

The 44th marched out of Silchar on the 21st
November to Luckipur, and ten Sappers left
in boats on the same day for Mynadhur. The
road, which, as far as Luckipur, is the high
road to Munipur, was very good, and from this
point to Alui tea-garden but few difficulties were
encountered. Beyond this, however, it lay
along the left bank of the river, crossing the
spurs before mentioned, rising and falling continually, often as much as seven hundred feet,
and always with a very steep gradient. Throughout its whole length there was not a single level
portion extending to the distance of one hundred
yards. It was altogether a most fatiguing and
harassing road—the march along which reminded
one of the old King of France, of whom we are
told, that " He, with all his men, marched up
the hill, to march down again."

The road, or rather path—for it never aspired to be anything more—lay through a jungle of fine forest trees, from the branches of which huge creepers hung in graceful festoons, with a profusion of tall bamboos and cane all around, while tangled thorns and shrubs, with a network of long roots, covered every inch of ground between these. Regarded as forest scenery, the aspect of the road was very fine; but to troops on the march, the irritation caused by its difficulties interfered materially with any appreciation of the beautiful in which they could indulge.

> " On either hand
> Uprose the trunks with underwood entwined,
> Making one thicket, thorny, dense, and blind,
> Where, with our axes, labouring half the day,
> We scarcely made some half a rod of way."

Compared with this route, I cannot help thinking that a little engineering would have made a better one over the Buban, and certainly a much shorter one. Afterwards, as we shall see at Chepui, laden elephants encountered and overcame the difficulties of a much worse path than that over the Buban, as it existed at first;

whereas the elephants, with their loads, could not be sent by the other road to Mynadhur, their burdens having to be taken on in boats.

As to the difficulty about water in the Buban, Captain Badgley, passing over with a survey party for the first time, to join the head-quarters, saw near the very highest points of the path a ravine in which his practised eye led him to suspect that the precious fluid might be found, and sending some of his men down into it, a stream was discovered within two hundred yards of the path, which afterwards sufficed at one time for the wants of more than four hundred coolies, without any sensible decrease in the supply. This fact renders it evident that if a survey party, " the pioneers of civilisation," had been allowed to precede the column as far as it could with safety, instead of remaining idle in Cachar for a month, great expense, and much loss of time, would have been saved.

In the meantime news had arrived in Cachar that the Coolie corps, under Captain Heydayat Ali, had been attacked by cholera at Kala Rokka; and Colonel Sheriff, 42nd Light Infantry, Major

Moore, with Drs. White and Gregg, were sent down to that camp. The medical and embarking authorities at Calcutta are stated to have protested against the crowding of eight hundred coolies into two flats, but their protest was of no avail. The coolies were neither accompanied by any European officer, nor had sufficient medical aid been provided for them. The ordinary precautions to prevent overcrowding, so strictly enforced in the case of labourers imported to work in the tea-gardens, seem to have been entirely disregarded; and the result was what might have been anticipated.

Dr. White, on his arrival, divided the coolies into three camps, at different points along the river. While the hospital remained at Kala Rokka, a convalescent camp was established some few miles further up the stream; but, notwithstanding these and other judicious measures, with the exertions of the medical officers, the disease was not got entirely under control till towards the end of December; by which time the number of the coolie corps was reduced to three hundred and eighty-seven.

A very serious strain was thus brought on the Commissariat Department, who were called on to supply carriage for the baggage of the troops, as well as for their own stores. Fortunately water-carriage was available as far as Tipai Mukh; and the collector of Sylhet undertook, in our emergency, to supply three hundred coolies to fill up the vacancies caused by the outbreak of cholera.

This incident is only one of the many examples we have had, in almost all our expeditions, of that inattention to details which is so conspicuous a defect in British arrangements, and was at no time more remarkable than in the Crimean war. In the present instance, it well nigh perilled the success of this Expedition at its very outset.

CHAPTER VIII.

MYNADHUR—THE TELEGRAPH—A DAILY POST ESTABLISHED—
ROUTE TO TIPAI MUKH—SCENERY ON THE BARAK—TRIAL
OF ELEPHANTS — ENCAMPMENT — THE GOORKHAS—VARIOUS
STATIONS—TIPAI MUKH—BRIDGE BUILT BY KOOKIES—A
NATIVE SAPPER—THE COMMISSARIAT FLEET OF BOATS—A
LUSHAI IDEA.

CHAPTER VIII.

MYNADHUR, the last and most outlying of the tea-gardens, is prettily situated on the left bank of the Barak, where the river, taking a semi-circular bend, leaves a long stretch of tolerably level ground between its banks and the foot of the hills. The garden covers several low tilas, the bungalow crowning one of them; and beneath this, on the river's bank, are the huts and bazaar of the coolie labourers. There is also a small stockade of ancient bamboos, the weakness and ruinous state of which sufficiently indicate the sense of security felt by the inhabitants of the garden, who, however, have a small police-guard generally stationed there. Though so far removed from all aid, this garden has never, I believe, been attacked by Lushais,

owing probably to the extreme difficulty of the
country between it and their own border.

The General and Staff arrived at Mynadhur,
about the 29th November, with one wing of the
44th and the Sappers. The jungle about
Mynadhur consisting principally of bamboo, no
difficulty was experienced in speedily constructing barracks, hospitals, magazines, godowns, and
officers' quarters.

Commissariat stores for three months had
been collected here, and ordnance and other stores
were arriving; while a fleet of small boats, of the
light tonnage necessary for passing the rapids and
shallows of the Barak higher up, had been sent
down from Sylhet and Cachar.

The boatmen in these districts had the most
intense horror of this part of the country, and it
was with great difficulty that they were induced
to go with their boats; many preferring to sink
them, while they themselves disappeared in some
place of concealment till the danger was past.

Meanwhile, the line of telegraph from Cachar
had been carried down to Mynadhur; the telegraph
party, under their energetic chief, having brought

it over the Buban, in the face of many obstacles.
A telegraph office was at once opened; and a
daily post was established between Silchar and
Mynadhur; so that by the first week in December,
the head-quarters of the Force were in communication with Calcutta, both by telegraph and post.

The road onwards to Tipai Mukh was at once
commenced, and some friendly Lushais having represented the best route to be on the Munipur
bank, the beginning of it was made on that side.

It may be necessary to explain the presence of
these Lushais in camp. Mr. Edgar, who was still
in Cachar, having sent messages to Sukpilal, was
anxiously awaiting their return. Eight Lushais
from Poiboi's villages arrived with presents, but
they were men of small account and not entrusted
with any definite overtures. They said that they
had met Raipa, an old Kookie who had been dispossessed by the Lushais, and who accompanied
the column as guide and interpreter. This Raipa
was then exploring to find a route, but these men
said to Mr. Edgar that he was not likely to find
one in the direction taken by him, but that they
knew of one by which they would guide the troops,

I

and four of them were sent down for that purpose.

The scenery all up the Barak is extremely beautiful, lofty wooded hills coming down to the water's edge, and receding here and there, so as to afford glimpses of more distant ranges, while large rocks and sandy strips diversify the character of the banks. The river winds about very much, the bends presenting a series of pictures, the elements of which, wooded hills, rocks, and water, though ever the same, are constantly varying in arrangement; and in the varieties of light and shade, each differs from the other in some point of detail, but on the whole all appear equally beautiful. Alligators bask in the sun here and there on the rocks, sliding off lazily into the deep pools beneath when a boat approaching too near rouses them from their slumbers.

As the head-quarters advanced, the regiments in rear followed up in order, each working on a certain portion of the road. The Artillery was left in Cachar till the road to Mynadhur was reported fit for elephants, and they did not get the order to march till the 2nd December.

The time, however, was not wasted; the ex-

periment of elephants instead of mules, as animals
of draught, was to be tried in this campaign; and
the gunners not having received their elephants
till their arrival in Cachar, they were fully employed in altering and refitting their equipment,
many portions of which were entirely novel and
untried. The strength of the battery was also
made up by drafts from the 42nd and 22nd regiments, and these had to be instructed in their new
work; but when the order for the march arrived
it found them all ready and in first rate order.

The road onwards from Mynadhur was similar
in character to that up to it, precipitous and
jungly. Four camps were established between
Mynadhur and Tipai Mukh. These camps were
numbered from one to four; a large board being
nailed up on a tall tree near the entrance to each,
with an inscription roughly painted in black,
"Station No. 1, &c."

A description of one will suffice for all, as well
as for many of the others formed south of Tipai
Mukh.

Arrived at the halting place, all the troops
went to work cutting down branches of trees and

bamboos, collecting leaves, grass, &c. In this work the active little Goorkhas of the 44th N. I., were much more at home than their up-country brethren in arms, who at first used to look helplessly on, while the former, springing into trees like monkeys, lopped off branches, collected bamboos, &c., and had quickly constructed comfortable ranges of cantos, with a low raised bamboo floor as a sleeping place, before the others had made up their minds what to do.

All the Sepoys had been supplied with kookries, a peculiar kind of native knife, most effective in cutting jungle when successfully used. The Goorkhas, as a rule, were possessed of their own, but those supplied by Government were soon useless, often breaking after the first few blows, efficiency having been sacrificed to economy.

A large number of Cachari, Mekir, and Kookie coolies were with the advance, and these men were very expert in cutting jungle and building huts. In an almost incredibly short space of time, they ran up quarters for the General and other officers with him. The framework was fastened together by strips of bark, and the walls consisted of

bamboo, leaves, and grass. Each hut was furnished with a standing bedstead, a table and stool
of bamboo. Outside was the mess-table, the super-
structure of which was formed of split bamboo,
supported by legs of rough timber; and around
it were seats constructed also of split bamboo.

It was astonishing how soon a waste, howling
wilderness of jungle was transformed into a
pleasant camp; and as abundance of fire-wood was
at hand, large camp-fires were always maintained,
which tended to keep these halting-places drier
and healthier than might have been expected.

All these stations were situated close to the
river's edge; a position by which an ample supply
of water was secured, and the Commissariat's
boats were able to provide the troops with the
necessary provisions every evening—the coolies
being thus set free for road-making. The rapids
proved passable for boats up to two hundred
maunds, though they were dragged through these
with difficulty.

At No. 3, the road again crossed to the Cachar
side, and so continued to Tipai Mukh. A floating
bridge of ingenious construction provided a con-

venient passage across the river at each of the
three points where the road changes from one side
to the other. The bridge consisted of an octagonal
raft of bamboo and matting, slung down stream
at two adjacent corners by large cane loops to a
very strong rope of cane ; which, firmly fastened
at each end to trees on either bank, hung slackly
in the water. The raft was worked backwards
and forwards by two men hauling the rope
through the loops.

General Bourchier reconnoitred Tipai Mukh in
person on the 9th, and notwithstanding predictions
to the contrary, no stockade or other demonstra-
tion of hostility was discovered. The place was
found to be admirably suited for a large camp
or dépôt.

It is situated, as its name implies, at the con-
fluence of the Tuivai (according to the Lushais,
miscalled Tipai by us) or Tipai with the Barak,
at the point where the latter, flowing in a south-
westerly direction through Munipur, takes a
sudden turn northward. At that season of the
year the Tuivai was reduced to a small stream of
about fifty yards in width, leaving on its southern

bank a large stretch of shingly beach, which, with a high sandy plateau, formed a square of some seven acres, bounded on the east and north by the Tuivai, west by the Barak, and south by a steep wooded hill, the end of a spur from a range to the south-west.

North of the Tuivai again, along the left bank of the Barak, was another long strip of sand and shingle, of some ten acres in extent. No doubt when the rains set in, the rivers, swollen and turbulent, rushing violently past their banks, and coming suddenly into collision, cover this bare space with a mass of seething waters; but in December, when they had sunk to quiet peaceable streams, it afforded us good dry camping ground.

On the south beach, Commissariat and Ordnance godowns were erected, and the Artillery and Engineer parks found accommodation, while, on the sandy plateau above, officers' quarters, mess, &c., were established.

On the northern strip, Hospitals and Sepoys' lines were built, sufficient space remaining for a camping ground for elephants; and a light bridge was thrown across the Tipai by the Cachari Kookies. Practical fellows these, caring little for mathematics and theory. While a scientific officer was calculating, in a hut close by, the strength of timber necessary for the bridge, the weight of troops likely to pass over it, the force of the current, and other considerations to which education and engineering books teach us to attach importance, as necessary to the safe construction of a bridge, these Kookies, who had never heard of Tredgold, and probably would not be any handier if they had, had actually built a bridge with the materials, small timber and bamboos, nearest to hand—a bridge built so substantially that it lasted throughout the campaign. When the aforesaid Engineer officer came out with his design and calculation, faultless, no doubt, in every detail, we may feel sure he looked rather surprised when he saw his work done for him.

I may here mention another amusing incident. Colonel Stafford and Captain Harvey, R.E., were talking to a soubadar of the 22nd, when the latter expressed his opinion that if the

Lushais only dammed up the Tipai a few miles above the camp, till a large volume of water had accumulated, and then let it out, it would sweep away the camp entirely.

Captain Harvey said, " Perhaps the soubadar will be good enough to explain the size of the dam, where it could be constructed to be out of the reach of our troops, and also the amount of water necessary for this work of annihilation."

Here his orderly, with the usual freedom of natives, joined in the conversation by saying, " Of what use is it asking the soubadar, Sahib, these questions, only we Sappers know all this kind of work."

Considering that a native Sapper knows very little, if anything, more than an ordinary Sepoy, this calm assumption of superiority was delicious.

A strong picquet was placed on the hill before mentioned, the trees cleared away, and a small field-work thrown up, at an elevation of two hundred feet above the camp, with which it communicated by a small zigzag trench, which it commanded, as well as a long reach of the Tipai, thus preventing the possibility of a surprise from the south.

A similar work was constructed on the hill to the north-east of the Tuivai, guarding against attack from that direction. The north end of the camp was further protected by a small trench and breastwork, extending across the strip of sand to the river's edge.

Of course all this laborious work was not accomplished at once, but to prevent confusion, I have described all these details here. The great disadvantage of this camp was that, lying low, surrounded by wooded hills rising above it to a height of twelve hundred feet, every evening as the sun sank behind the western hills, fog and mist slowly settled down upon it, and did not lift till late next morning.

The day after the General made his appearance at Tipai Mukh, a fleet of two hundred boats, laden with stores under the command of Mr. Patch, District Superintendent of Sylhet Police, and escorted by some of the 44th, also arrived.

Mr. Patch's services had been placed specially at the disposal of the Military authorities, and throughout the Expedition he continued to command this Commissariat Fleet, a duty involving hard and monotonous work, which was little likely to be varied by any excitement; but on the able and zealous performance of which depended much of the success of the Expedition, and this ability and zeal were not wanting.

Having advanced so far, the next thing to be done was to find the onward path and convert it into a road. The General and Colonel Roberts, under the guidance of a Lushai, attempted to explore a road towards Kholel, but it was exceedingly steep and rocky. One of the Lushais then in camp, a Muntri of Poiboi, Darpong by name, stated that if it was made worth his while he might be able to find a better way. Mr. Edgar arrived at Tipai Mukh on the 12th December, and hearing what Darpong had said, sent him and Raipa to explore the country.

Mr. Edgar, after his arrival, advised the General to push on to Kholel for the following reasons. While they remained at Tipai, they had not the opportunity of opening communications with friendly or neutral tribes, which

would be afforded by occupying Kholel, situated
as it was between the villages of Khalsom, Lalhi,
and Sinpaun on the one side, and Poiboi's on
the other; all of which were supposed to come
under one or other of the above classifications.

An idea had also become prevalent among the
Lushais that the force would never get beyond
Tipai Mukh; but would remain there till negotiations were entered into, or some of the tribes
submitted. It therefore seemed of great importance that an onward move should be made, to
convince the Lushais that we really meant to
go through their country, and also to force them
to adopt some decisive policy towards us.

It was therefore determined to advance on
the 16th. A working party had been sent on the
14th to a point about two and a half miles along
the elephant track pointed out by Darpong,
where was a level piece of ground with two small
streams running through it. Here our party
camped and set to work on improving the track,
and thither the head-quarters proceeded on
the 16th.

As the road had to be explored each day, and

the next day's camp ahead settled beforehand,
the advance was necessarily slow. The road, as
far as the Senvong range, followed a tolerably
easy gradient, and lay through slightly less difficult jungle than had been previously encountered.
The principal difficulties which impeded its construction arose from the very rocky character
of the hill in several places, which necessitated
a good deal of blasting. Water was met with
in several places.

CHAPTER IX.

———

VILLAGE SITES—RUMOURS—DARPONG—THE SENVONG RANGE—
FIRST VIEW OF THE LUSHAI COUNTRY—EXTRAORDINARY HILL
—SYMBOLIC WARNINGS TO THE TROOPS—WEIR FOR CATCHING
FISH—ATTEMPTS TO STOP THE ADVANCE—A SKIRMISH—
CHRISTMAS DAY.

CHAPTER IX.

STATION No. 5 was situated on the site of an old Kookie village about five miles from Tipai Mukh, and No. 6 near the top of the Senvong range, six miles further on.

This last station was reached on the 19th. Fragrant limes, cinnamon, and walnut trees were found on the sites of the old villages; the limes were a pleasing addition to our hot rum and water after dinner. The village sites passed on the way to No. 6 had belonged to Kookies, and had been deserted in consequence of the aggressions of the Lushais. The latter had not occupied them, as they were too near our frontier. As our cultivated territory advanced south, the Lushais seem gradually to have withdrawn, keeping the boundary line of their villages and culti-

K

vation nearly parallel to that of ours, a belt of impenetrable jungle intervening.

On the 18th some Lushais were met with, who ran away, but shortly after the exploring party came up again with some of them, who said they were Kholel men.

Two of these returned to camp in the evening; and from their statements it appeared that a large number of Lushais were collected at the Tuibum. These they represented as friendly, but from a remark made by one of them, it was gathered that they had received orders to oppose our progress. The Lushais also said a party of a hundred and fifty men had gone in the direction of the Bubans. Notice of this was at once sent back to Tipai Mukh and Mynadhur, with orders to the commanders at those places to warn all survey and telegraph parties.

In the evening, Darpong and the others asked to be allowed to return to their villages. They evidently expected that a collision would surely take place between us and the Lushais, and were afraid to be found in our camp when such an event should happen.

The General, thinking nothing was to be gained by keeping them against their will, decided to let them go; a decision attended, as we shall see hereafter, with the happiest results.

These men left on the 19th, charged with messages to their people, to the effect that our object was to recover the captives taken by Lalboora and Tangdong, and that we had no quarrel with the people of Poiboi or Lalhi, so long as they refrained from molesting us.

A halt was made on the 20th, in order to get up supplies, and reconnoitre the route onwards. The old route to Kholel was found to have been closed by the Lushais; but another, along the ridge of the hill, was said to lead straight to Vanbong. This latter route turned out to be a very good one, and a camping-ground with good water was discovered at the top of a spur leading to the Tuibum.

The Senvong range is a long, lofty spur, its average elevation being nearly four thousand feet above the level of the sea. It is tolerably open, having once been extensively cultivated, but the old jooms are now covered with long grass.

From the higher points of this range, the first extensive views of the Lushai country were obtained. Far away to the north-east, stretched the Munipur ranges; to the east, the distant Lushai hills, rising above the lower and nearer ranges; some clothed in every variety of green, while in others the forest was broken and relieved by the warm tints of masses of sandstone and red clay, of which these hills consist.

About fourteen miles to the south-east, a great round-looking mass, sending out long, level spurs, stood up, brown and bare, from the countless jooms upon its face; and on the spurs north and south, appeared the villages of Tingridum and Chepui; the gabled ends of new bamboo houses glistening in the sun like little whited temples.

Behind these, rose the high and rugged ranges known as Surklang, Muthilen, and Lengteng; while nearer, appeared the high Kholel Range, on a bare ridge of which we could still discover the site of Voupilal's great village; and nearer still, across the valley of Tuivai, and hiding the hills to the south, was the Vanbong hill, a large level mass, with broad sloping spurs, cleared of a good

deal of the forests for the jooms and villages of
the people who had lately removed thither from
Kholel on the death of Voupilal.

Between Kholel and Vanbong, looking down
the valley of the Tipai, the scene was closed by
an extraordinary hill, called Momrang, sloping
gradually away on the east, but ending towards
the west in an abrupt precipice, and forming an
excellent landmark; while on the west, the ranges
of Rengtipahar, Noonvai, &c., rose one above the
other, till lost in the haze of the far off horizon;
and here and there in the valleys below glistened
the silvery bends of the Tuivai and its affluents.

On the 22nd, the head-quarters, with Mr.
Edgar and Colonel Nuthall's wing of the 44th,
descended to the Tuibum stream. This was a
difficult and trying march, the spur being very
steep, and the jungle thick bamboo, especially
near the river.

In several places the Lushais had put up some
symbols, intended as warnings to the troops not
to advance. One was a small model of a gallows,
made of bamboos, with rough pieces of wood
intended to represent men hanging from it; and

another consisted of small strips of bamboo stuck into the trunk of a felled tree, from the wounds of which, a deep red sap, strongly resembling blood, exuded — indicating to the troops the fate that awaited them if they persisted in the advance.

At the spot where the path comes out on the Tuibum, was a weir made of bamboo and stones for catching fish, and on the opposite bank was a bamboo watch-house raised some twelve feet from the ground. On this weir, and beneath this house, some forty or fifty Lushais were collected. They yelled out to our men to turn back, and made threatening demonstrations. It was explained to them, as before, that no harm was intended them if they offered no opposition to our advance, and that our path led us that way, and the General was determined to follow it; the General moreover ordered the 44th not to fire unless attacked first.

The advance was then continued over the weir, and the Lushais retired without firing, but still shouting. As we proceeded onwards we soon came to another bend of the river, where it had to be forded. Here ensued another parley, the Lushais wishing us to wait where we were, and their Muntries would be sent in to the General.

These attempts to stop the advance were repeated without success at each ford till at last the Tuivai itself was crossed, and the Lushais disappeared. The force encamped on the bank of the Tuivai, near its junction with the Tuibum.

In the evening a reinforcement of fifty men of the 22nd, under Major Stafford, arrived; and the next day, the 23rd, it was determined, by marching on Kholel, to give the Lushais no opportunity of strengthening their position if they wished to fight. So leaving a guard in camp, the General took the rest of his force up the hill.

The ascent was through thick jungle, and very steep. Colonel Roberts was in front with the advanced guard, and as he arrived at the edge of the joom, a Kookie constable , named Panek, pointed out that there were some Lushais in the joom-house. The Colonel then waited to get the men together, a matter of considerable difficulty, owing to the narrowness of the path.

As the foremost skirmishers debouched upon

the joom, they were received by a volley from
the Lushais, by which Panek was dangerously
wounded. The 22nd then charged, and the
Lushais fired one more volley and disappeared
over the crest of the hills above.

The joom-house was found to be full of grain,
which was at once destroyed, and the little force
continued its toilsome ascent, driving the Lushais
from joom to joom. The tactics adopted by the
latter were to post themselves at the top of each
steep ascent, in positions commanding the entrance
to the jooms, and as the foremost men came out
into the open, to fire a volley at them and disappear into the heavy jungle.

Of course their style of fighting, the steep-
ness of the hillside, and the denseness of the forest,
all favoured the Lushais, and were against us.
From frequent traces of blood found about, it was
tolerably evident that the enemy did suffer much
loss ; but of course it was impossible to ascertain its
extent, as the Lushais have a superstition that if
the head of a man slain in battle falls into the
hands of his enemy, the man himself becomes the
slave of the victor in the next world ; and conse-

quently they will make any effort to carry off their dead and wounded, or to conceal them till the enemy has retired. On the other hand they spare no pains, and often fear no danger, in the endeavour to obtain the heads of their enemies.

Storehouses full of grain were found in each joom, which were all destroyed; and after skirmishing up the hill for about three hours, two villages recently constructed were reached and burnt down. A third, near which a stream of water was found, the General determined to occupy, and he sent back to the camp on the Tuivai for the baggage; in the meantime continuing the march to Kalhi's chief village, which had been seen from Senvong, and was near the summit of the Vanbong ridge. It was at last discovered at a height of three thousand three hundred feet above the camp of the morning.

The Lushais made an attempt to defend the village, but the 44th drove them out, losing two men in the assault. The village was then burnt, and the troops returned to the one previously fixed upon for occupation. Shortly after their arrival the Lushais commenced firing

into the camp from the forest which surrounded
it closely, and wounded a sentry of the 22nd.
Two other men of this regiment had also been
wounded, one dangerously, in the course of the
skirmishing.

Doolies, a kind of canvas hammock slung on
a long pole, and carried on the shoulders of a
couple of coolies, always accompanied the troops,
for the conveyance of the wounded.

Shots were exchanged between the Lushais
and our sentries all through the night. Two
flint-locks were picked up in the morning near
the left picket, and the ground all round was
stained with blood.

Major Stafford patrolled down to the camp on
the Tuivai to get up supplies, skirmishing with
the enemy each way.

The General also, with Colonel Roberts and a
party of the 44th, under Captain Robertson, went
out to another village to the south. This was
carried at a rush by the Goorkhas, and shared
the fate of the villages on the previous day. In
this affair only one man was wounded.

While this was going on, some of the troops

CHRISTMAS DAY.   139

left in camp were employed in clearing the jungle round the village, a work which was attended with good results; as the Lushais, deprived of cover close to the sentries, did not annoy them much during the night.

The next day—Christmas Day—the 44th went out again, under Captains Lightfoot and Robertson, and burnt some twenty well-filled granaries, They secured the body and gun of one Lushai, which were sent into camp. The casualties on their side were four men wounded, one of whom was badly hit in the forehead.

Major Stafford also patrolled down to the lower camp and back again, fighting each way.

The Kookies in camp were greatly excited when the Lushai's body was taken in, and were very anxious to cut off his head, but of course they were not allowed to do so. Old Raipa, on finding that he could not have his desire upon his enemy, set up a dismal wail which must have been heard for miles.

In the evening all the officers assembled at the head-quarter mess, to keep up as far as possible the semblance of Christmas. They sat at a table raised in a conspicuous position, with candles burning before them, and Lushais firing from the jungle close by.

Whether from some idea that the death of a white man would be more severely revenged than that of a Sepoy, or from some superstitious notion, it is impossible to say ; but notwithstanding the excellent mark which the dinner-table and its lights presented to them, no shots were fired in that direction, though single sentries posted quite near to it were hit.

Another curious fact is that, when some songs were sung after dinner, the Lushais stopped firing altogether while the singing lasted, commencing again when the song was over.

While occupying this village, it was discovered that the path which would take us in the direction of Lalboora passed by old Kholel, and that consequently a mistake had been made in coming up to the new Kholel villages. It was therefore determined to retire to the weir across the Tuibum, where were Colonel Stafford's wing of the 22nd and the Sappers, and seek for the path thence to Poiboi.

Moreover, the village which we then occupied was not tenable for any length of time, the Lushais getting daily more wary and skilful; and being favoured by the jungle they made the camp too hot for our troops.

Two shots closely following each other, and invariably coming from the same spot, induced the idea that one of the Lushais was armed with a double-barrelled gun, and was a better marksman than his fellows. It was found afterwards, however, that two men, brothers, hunted together. We also learned subsequently that one of them was killed in a skirmish, and no more was heard of the double barrel.

On the 26th, when it was determined to return to the Tuibum a Goorkha, Robertson's orderly, was shot through the heart as he was rolling up the bedding from which his master had just risen, in a house in the midst of the village.

As the return to the weir must have looked to the Lushais very much like a retreat, it was necessary to keep them in ignorance of that movement as long as possible, and by occupying their attention prevent them from following their usual

tactics of lying in wait for the long string of
coolies and followers, and firing into it.

The retreat was executed most successfully and
skilfully. The 22nd formed the advance. The
baggage and sick were sent on in front, under
the protection of some of the 44th, distributing
a couple of files between the coolies at short
intervals. The remainder of the 44th formed
the rear-guard, and were accompanied by the
General himself, and Colonel Roberts.

The day was bright and clear, the air crisp
and cold, and below in the valley lay the soft
white mist, as the first detachment moved out
of the village. The 22nd had, as before mentioned, patrolled down to the Tuivai for two days
in the same manner, and did not excite any notice
on the part of the Lushais, who were busily engaged in exchanging shots with the picquets. The
coolies were thus all got safely out of the camp ;
the picquets were driven in, and the village fired
by a party of Kookies. The Lushais then discovered the manœuvre, but too late, for the
coolies were well ahead, and the rear-guard was
between them. They tried, however, wherever the

nature of the ground gave them a chance, to get by the rear-guard and attack the coolies; but they were baffled by the Goorkhas, "who," in the words of one of the staff-officers present, "extending rapidly where the ground allowed, retired through their supports as if on parade." The troops were admirably led by Colonel Nuthall and Captain Robertson.

CHAPTER X.

TEMPORARY CESSATION OF HOSTILITIES—THE LUSHAI AC-
COUNT OF THE KHOLEL AFFAIR—DIFFICULTY OF COMMUNI-
CATING WITH THE NATIVES—A GUIDE FOR THE SURVEY
OFFICERS—THE MUNIPUR CONTINGENT—POIBOI'S PRESENTS—
EVENTS AT TIPAI MUKH—LUSHAI ATTACK.

L

CHAPTER X.

THE Tuibum was reached without a single casualty, a few granaries, which had escaped during the advance, being destroyed on the way.

The camp was formed on a level piece of ground of some extent, close to the fishing weir, and a picquet left during the night, in a small stockade at the Tuivai camp, was withdrawn the next day. This Tuibum encampment was surrounded on all sides by steep hills, as usual covered with forest, and the Lushais, concealed among the trees, continued to annoy us by firing into it, and at the working parties. The casualties, however, were not numerous, only a coolie and a sapper being wounded.

The route onward was explored on the 27th, and it was found that it ascended the hill soon after leaving the weir, leading up a steep and narrow spur of a hill called Pabarchung.

On the 28th the troops remained in camp, and were joined by Colonel Rattray and his wing of the 42nd A L.D. On the 29th, the General, taking these with him, and accompanied by Captain Badgley, went back to the burnt villages.

The principal object of this Expedition was to show the Lushais that, though the force had retired from that particular hill, they were by no means to conclude that it could not return to it, for that till they (the Lushais) made submission they would get no peace.

As soon as the detachment left the camp, it was fired into from all sides, and one man was slightly wounded.

Coming out on to a joom, after ascending the hill for some little distance, the foremost of the party saw some Lushais, who fired at them and disappeared, not without the loss of one of their number, whom they carried off, leaving his musket, cloth, &c., where he fell.

Near the first village burnt on the 23rd, as the leading skirmisher was making his way along a

narrow path, a man wearing a yellow cloak and
waving a red puggree appeared suddenly before
him. Fortunately Captain Butler, who was just
behind, recognised him as Darpong, and stopped
the advance till the General and Mr. Edgar went
up to the front and heard what he had to say;
which was that he had been sent by Poiboi to
stop hostilities at Kholel, and to make peace for
the villages, and that Poiboi's brother was on his
way to make terms for their own villages.

The General consented to a temporary cessation of hostilities; and when he understood this,
Darpong climbed up into a dead tree, sounded the
cry of peace to the invisible foes in the jungle,
and from that moment all firing ceased. Then
going on to the village, Mr. Edgar proceeded to
arrange preliminaries with Darpong. The latter
promised that all firing should stop along our
route, and that our communications should be
kept open for us, a promise which was most
religiously kept; for though on that afternoon
Colonel Davidson was fired at a few miles out of
camp, on his way to Tipai Mukh, by some Lushais
who could not then have got news of the truce,

yet with this exception the roads were from that moment perfectly safe for dâk-runners, coolies bringing up supplies, &c.

Captain Badgley went to the top of the hill and took some observations, and then the party returned to camp.

While at the village, a great many Lushais were hanging about afraid to approach their late enemies; but some officers went out to meet them; and some

> " A little of us by our signs did learn,
> Then went their way, and so at last all fear
> Was laid aside, and thronging they drew near,
> To look upon us—"

and upon our swords and revolvers, which they examined with great interest.

The General remained at the Tuibum camp till the 6th January, this delay being necessary in order to get up sufficient supplies for a further advance, as, in the rapid march on Kholel, these had been overrun, as well as to complete the communications with Tipai Mukh; the time was spent in getting up these supplies, and commencing the road over Pabarchung, and by Mr. Edgar in

constant interviews with the representatives of
the north and north-eastern Lushais.

Mr. Edgar tells us that the following is the
Lushai version of the Kholel business, as far as
he could learn it from themselves. It will be remembered I mentioned, in a former chapter, that
Voupilal's people were divided, after his death,
in their allegiance between his widow and mother;
the former of whom lives at Vanbong (New
Kholel). When our advance was made on Kholel
the adherents of the latter, being generally
the older people of the tribe, remembered the
fate of their villages in Colonel Lister's Expedition,
and wished to make a show at any rate of friendship, in order to get on to Poiboi in the East, and
away from them—while the other and younger
party wished to oppose and advance, and dwelt
on the fact that in 1849 the force had to hurry
out of the country.

On the other hand, if the Kholel people opposed
us unsuccessfully, there was danger of all their
villages to the west being attacked, and it was
equally Poiboi's interest to keep us, if possible,
from reaching his territory. This would account

for the Lushais' remark at No. 6, that the people of Vanbong had been ordered to oppose our advance at the Tuibum.

" The two parties do not seem to have come to any decision, but probably there was a tacit compromise that if we did not attempt to visit Vanbong we should not be opposed, and that in this case the Kholel people would keep on outwardly friendly terms with us, unless we met with some disaster ahead, when they might fall upon us with perfect safety.

" Of course it would have been impossible for us to accept such a situation. It was almost a necessity for us to make every village behind safe before taking a step in advance. From the position of the New Kholel group of villages it could have done us more injury than any other, and we could not make sure of it without visiting it and leaving a party in a position to command all the villages."

The Lushais say that they did not intend to provoke hostilities on the 23rd; but that the rashness of some of their youths committed them to the attack, and then all were compelled to unite in order to get rid of us.

In the return of the troops to Tuibum, leaving some of the villages still standing, they recognised, as they thought, a similar proceeding to that of Colonel Lister, and expected we were now about to leave the country. The people began therefore to re-occupy their houses and bring back their families from the various places of safety to which they had been sent, and also to harass our communications. Contrary to their expectations, however, when they saw General Bourchier marching towards their villages again on the 29th, instead of retiring as fast as possible on Tipai Mukh, a panic seized them; and a village council being hastily held, instant submission was urged. The Western people also advised the same step, and those whose villages had been destroyed, were compelled to yield with a bad grace.

Then came the difficulty of communicating with us, but Darpong undertook the risk, with what result we have already seen. Three of the Kholel people were given as hostages, to remain with us till our return. These men accompanied us throughout the Expedition, and did very good service on several occasions. One of them named

Santong, the survivor of tho two sharp-shooting brothers, could speak a little Hindustani, and he was appointed as guide to the survey party, and used to accompany it to point out the various hills, &c. ; and this he always did, cheerfully rendering material assistance to the survey officers.

The establishment of the posts at Bongkong and Koloshib caused these Western Lushais great uneasiness, and it appeared that the advance of the Munipur contingent was influencing for good those to the east. Much anxiety was felt by the General, lest this contingent advancing so far south should actually come into collision with the Eastern tribes, as such an encounter was far from desirable, whatever its immediate result might be, and messengers were despatched to General Nuthall explaining General Bourchier's wishes.

On the 18th January matters were finally settled with the Kholel men, and some commissaries were sent to Khalkom desiring him to join.

On the 5th, some of Poiboi's men brought in a pig and some fowls, &c., as presents, with assurances of Poiboi's desire to keep on friendly terms with us. They reported that Darpong had not returned from his journey to General Nuthall, but that no fighting had, as yet, taken place between their people and the Munipuris, though the latter were then close to Chiboo.

Before continuing the narrative of the advance, it will be necessary to return to Tipai Mukh, where an event had occurred which had startled that little garrison out of the fancied security they had been enjoying. The troops at that time, at Tipai Mukh, were the Artillery, a wing of the 42nd, under Colonel Sheriff, and Colonel Hicks' wing of the 44th, the whole being under command of the latter officer.

The days were passed very quietly in erecting godowns, improving the defences, and fishing. Some very fine mahaseer were caught with spoon-bait. Two officers took ninety-one pounds of fish between them in one day, and Captain R. Cookesley, R.A., the day after caught five fish, weighing in all eighty-two pounds, the largest turning the scale at twenty-one and a half pounds.

The news from the front used generally to come in during the night, and was discussed the following morning, during the usual early tea and biscuit over the big camp fire.

Sometimes the Commissariat had a baking day, and a loaf was served out to each officer. On such occasions long bamboo toasting-forks were cut, and the pleasure of making one's own toast was much appreciated.

On Christmas Day some beeves arrived from Mynadhur, after a most adventurous journey, the rafts in which they were having been twice upset in the rapids, and they had to swim for their lives. They were slightly lean, but after tinned mutton were most welcome; and some of the freshly caught mahaseer, this beef, and a whole bottle of beer to each man, formed, as times then were with us, a very fine Christmas dinner, after which we tried to emulate the usual festivities of the season with a brew of hot grog and a few old songs.

The Artillery and Commissariat elephants were usually sent a little way up the Tipai to graze, but on the morning of the 27th, the mahouts had incautiously taken thirty-six elephants further than they ought; and about 10 o'clock one of them ran into camp, apparently greatly terrified, shouting out that the elephants had been attacked by Lushais, their attendants killed, and the animals driven away up stream.

The alarm was at once given, and the troops fell in, though, from the mahout's incoherent manner and confused statements, his tale did not meet, at first, with full credence; but an elephant, with blood running from seven bullet wounds, appeared almost immediately to prove his story, which further information confirmed, with the addition that the Lushais, numbering about two hundred, were on their way to attack the camp.

The guns were at once placed in position at the east corner of the camp, commanding the Tuivai, and the picquets re-inforced.

These arrangements had just been carried out, when a few shots from the jungle on the opposite bank informed us of the vicinity of the enemy. Immediately afterwards, a volley was fired from the picquet on the top of the hill at some figures, seen for a second, passing through the jungle below.

Some officers passing up the left bank to reconnoitre, were fired at, a bullet nearly finding
its billet in one of them. To all the shots fired
by the invisible enemy, the troops responded by
volleys, with what effect of course could not be
known. At length a single shot from our side,
fired at a puff of smoke from the enemy's, was
followed by groans and cries in Hindustani,
upon which the firing ceased.

A party of the 42nd, under Captain Harrison,
accompanied by Captain Blackwood, having
crossed the Tuivai in boats, proceeded up the
river in search of the elephants, and were followed by a party of gunners in boats. The
former had gone about half a mile, when a
mahout crawled out of the jungle, with two gun-
shot wounds and a spear cut in his left leg and
foot. He said that while the mahouts and coolies
were loading the elephants with the grass, &c.,
they were suddenly surprised by about fifty
Lushais, who, having fired a volley from the
jungle, suddenly with a loud yell rushed out
upon them with spears and daôs, killing several.
He himself was sitting on his elephant when he

was wounded, and falling off into the long grass crept away unperceived, and concealed himself till he heard the approach of the Sepoys. He was sent at once into camp, and his wounds attended to ; one bullet was extracted, a piece of iron beaten into a slug of irregular shape.

Proceeding onwards, the party in search of the elephants came upon a few near the scene of the attack, and some of the mahouts who had also managed to escape the fury of the Lushais, on hearing our men, came out and took charge of the animals.

Towards evening the party returned, having succeeded in recovering nine. They also brought a Lushai gourd, cloth and bag, which they had picked up in the jungle whence the enemy had been firing in the morning. They, however, saw nothing whatever of the Lushais, who had disappeared as suddenly as they had come.

Everyone expected that the camp would be fired into during the night, and all lights and fires were ordered to be put out at an early hour. Several times during the evening, young hands heard, as they thought, the sound of gunshots;

but the more experienced laughed and explained that this noise was caused by the popping of bamboo in the camp fire. The air between the knots expands with the heat, and the bamboo bursts with a bang, exactly resembling the report of a gun.

Everything, however, passed off quietly till about two o'clock in the morning, when a cry was raised of "Lushai," and the whole force turned out at once. It was soon, however, discovered that the alarm was caused by a stampede among the elephants, about eighty of which were picketed to the north of the camp. One of them, with his forelegs hobbled, went galloping through the 44th camp, and the mahouts on perceiving him raised the alarm. Everyone soon turned in again.

Early next morning detachments of the Artillery and 42nd, under Captains Cookesley and Harrison, proceeded up the river in boats, and recovered all but three of the missing elephants. The former officer says :—

"The jungle along the banks was one tangled mass of coarse rank grass, varied by stretches

of shingly beach, covered here and there with
a hardy shrub, the roots of which are interlaced
in a manner to puzzle the best equestrian, but
through this the elephants were tracked with un-
erring precision by the sharp little Goorkhas."

The party also discovered and brought back to
camp the remains of three of the poor fellows who
had been killed by the Lushais. They presented
a ghastly spectacle, their bodies having been
hacked and mutilated in a most shocking manner;
their heads had been cut off, but not carried
away, only the scalps being taken. One of the
unfortunates was an old man, and his arms and
hands had been cut to pieces, apparently in attempting to ward off the cruel blows of his murderers.

While clearing the jungle near the picquet on the
hill, a spear-head was picked up, cut nearly in two
by an Enfield bullet; it must have been knocked
off the staff while in the hand of its owner, who
had a narrow escape.

I do not think it was ever known to which tribe
the men belonged who committed this attack,
though an idea gained some credence that Khalkom
was the leader, and that he was wounded in this

affair. Another rumour attributed the attack to the party returning from Monierkhal, of whose excursion northward notice had been sent from No. 6, as before mentioned.

This was the first and last excitement for those at Tipai Mukh, who thenceforth, to the close of the Expedition, pursued the even tenor of their way uninterruptedly.

The telegraph was completed as far as Tipai Mukh by the 31st December. The wing of the 42nd which had been working on the last bit of road into camp, which was very difficult and rocky, had been withdrawn when the fighting commenced in front, and this part was not finished for some time—the last stage of the journey being performed by water.

CHAPTER XI.

PROGRESS OF THE HEAD-QUARTERS—AT WORK ON THE ROAD—
A DESERTED VILLAGE—UNCOMFORTABLE NIGHT—AN EMIS-
SARY FROM SUKPILAL—THE CAMP AT CHEPUI—POIBOIS—
THE SENIVAI—GUARD VILLAGES—THE KHOLEL RANGE.

CHAPTER XI.

W^E may now accompany the head-quarters on the onward march for the rest of the campaign, as a passing reference to events occurring in rear is all that will be necessary.

All the wounded were sent in to Tipai Mukh on the 1st of January, to be attended at the dépôt hospital there.

Captain Harvey with his Sappers left Tuibum on the 4th for Pabarchung; and encamping near its summit, commenced work upon the road. Colonel Nuthall with his Goorkhas went into a beautiful little stream called the Tuitu, on the other side of the hill, and worked backwards to meet the Sappers.

The General and staff left Tuibum on the 6th, and halting at the Sapper camp for the night

arrived at Tuitu (No. 8.) early on the morning
of the 7th.

The Tuitu runs along a deep and narrow valley,
separating the Kholel range from Pabarchung. It
is a clear stream, with firm sandy and stony bed,
its banks clothed with bamboo, and a tall graceful
feathering reed.

On the way over Pabarchung a very good view
of the Vanbong hills was obtained, and many
more villages and innumerable jooms became
visible. These had been concealed from other
and nearer points of view by the denseness of the
forest, but now we could see the whole eastern
face of the hill. The elevation of the camp of
the Tuibum was seven hundred feet, the height
of Pabarchung three thousand seven hundred
feet, and the Tuitu, at the point we crossed it,
about one thousand five hundred feet.

On the 8th the Sappers having come up, the
whole moved on to the site of a deserted village,
called Daidoo, on the Kholel ridge, and were succeeded at No. 8 by the 22nd N. I.

The path led us through deserted jooms up a
steep and narrow spur. As we ascended, leaving

the region of bamboo behind, the jungle became more open, only grass and a few low shrubs growing between the tall trees. Wild heliotrope and cocoa-nuts, and other flowering weeds, abounded along the path.

The troops arrived at Daidoo between two and three, P.M., and a spot being fixed on for a camp, everyone was soon busy—some searching for water, others building huts. The water was found after a great search, but yielded a very insufficient supply.

This village had been deserted for some two years, and the stream was choked up with dead leaves, old bamboo, ashes, mud, &c., and though attempts were made to improve it by cleaning it and constructing small troughs, yet the result was far from satisfactory.

The sky had become clouded during the march, and there was no doubt that we should have rain, which came down heavily about six p.m., and lasted through the night.

Time and the friendly bamboo both being wanting, the huts were not successfully constructed and the rain came through in every part.

Very few had been fortunate enough to get mai-
châus constructed, and almost everyone passed
the greater part of the night in a swamp of
sloppy blankets and grass.

About seven o'clock next morning the rain and
mist cleared off, and the sun came out warm
and bright, accompanied by a keen strong wind,
blowing right across the ridge on which we were
encamped ; and availing ourselves of these two
beneficent agencies, our wet clothes and soaked
blankets were hung on ropes and stretched from
tree to tree, and soon dried.

Two theories were held by rival parties in the
camp, as to the best way of stretching a waterproof
sheet, whether outside over the leaf roof or inside
under it. The theories were put to the proof on
this occasion, and resulted in the triumph of the
first named, though some continued, against their
better judgment, to adhere to their old plan.

It must be evident, or ought to be, that the
sheet put outside keeps the water from penetrating through the leaves, conducting it off the sloping roof to the ground outside, while, if stretched
inside, no matter how tightly the stretching is

done, the rain, unless the sheet is arranged
at a very steep slope indeed, soon finds its way
through the leaves, and passes and collects gradually in the sheet, which becomes a reservoir of
water, liable on the slightest incautious touch to
discharge its contents in every direction within
the hut.

It is not a pleasant thing in a dark night, as
I found by experience, to have to get up about
two a.m., and stand under the dripping roof, to
empty out a gallon of icy-cold and dirty water,
which has bagged the sheet down to within a
foot of one's head. One occupant of our hut,
doing this without proper caution, sent the whole
of the collected water in a gush on to an unof-
fending fellow sleeping next to him, who,
having taken the precaution of putting his sheet
outside, would have otherwise remained dry
throughout the night. At the very best, the
inside arrangement, even if it does not carry all
the water on to the bed of the sleeper beneath,
makes the ground within the hut wet.

The next day, the 9th January, Mr. Edgar's
scouts informing him that a better supply of

water was to be found at Pachui, another deserted village about a mile off on the same range,
the General and staff with the 44th marched to
that place, leaving the Sappers at Daidoo to complete the road between Pachui and the Tuitu.

After his arrival at Pachui (known officially as
No. 9), Nura Sinpanu's muntri, and Rution Singh,
an emissary from Sukpilal, came in. The latter
is a Hindustani, formerly a coolie in a tea-garden,
who deserted to the Lushais some years back,
and has since acquired some influence among
the Western tribes, which he is supposed to have
frequently exercised to our prejudice.

They said that Khalkom was ill, and that
Sukpilal had gone to see him, but that they
would come in at once if the General would for-
give the delay.

They were sent back with the reply that, if
they wanted to see the General at Pachui, they
must come in at once, as the march would not be
delayed on their account. The Khalkom villages
were said to be three days' journey from No. 9.

Darpong also arrived with the letter he was to
have taken to General Nuthall. He said that, in

consequence of some ill-treatment Poiboi's messengers to General Nuthall had met with at the
hands of the Munipuris, the Lushais were afraid
to take this letter. Mr. Edgar considered this
story to be false, and believed that the real reason
for their not taking the letter, was the fear that
it might contain an order for an immediate attack
on the Lushais.

The camp at Pachui was admirably situated, as
it not only commanded the road to the Tuivai,
and southern portion of the valley and villages of
New Kholel, but also the country to the west,
where stood Khalkom's villages. At the same
time it covered the communications with Tuibum.

It was therefore determined to halt here, while
trying to bring the Western tribes to terms, and
collecting sufficient supplies to march rapidly on
Poiboi's village, if he should eventually declare
against us, and oppose our advance against Lal-
bura.

The onward road was at first to have been
made along the Kholel ridge, without going near
Poiboi; but we were told that a good route to Lal-
bura lay through the country of the Poibois, and as

there was a scarcity of water along the former, and Poiboi's intentions were so exceedingly doubtful, the General felt it necessary, in order to secure his communications, to pass through that chief's territory, and a road was accordingly commenced down to the Tuivai.

Poiboi had, on several occasions, expressed to Mr. Edgar his friendly feelings towards us, and his displeasure at the conduct of his cousins. Still it was not to be forgotten that it was against his own relations that the arms of the left column were directed; and as he could at any time himself assemble a large number of fighting men, he was informed that he must give a most satisfactory guarantee of his perfect neutrality.

Pachui is, as before mentioned, in the Kholel range, and the hill of Chepui just opposite to it. A deep valley intervenes, through which flows the Tuivai, some two thousand feet below, the elevation of Pachui camp being about three thousand eight hundred and fifty feet above sea level.

On the slopes of Chepui were visible the two large villages of Chepui and Tingridum, the most northerly of Poiboi's villages.

After Colonel Lister's Expedition in 1869, the Lushais withdrew their villages further south, leaving a large belt of jungly hills between themselves and our most southern cultivated tracts, and established what they called guard-villages, commanding the approach from our frontier to their chief villages. Daidoo and Pachui were the guard-villages to the chief's residence in Old Kholel, which will be described further on; and Chepui and Tingridum were the guard-villages to Poiboi's country, and his residence at Chetam; the range on which the latter is built being concealed from our view at Kholel by the lofty intervening range of Lengteng.

The Kholel range consists of a series of lofty peaks connected by narrow ridges. The peaks increase in height towards the south; the highest we reached, from which we observed angles, &c., was five thousand two hundred feet.

The Tuivai flows on three sides, separating the range from Momrang on the south, and Vanbong on the west; nearly opposite No. 9, the Tuivai flows out from the eastern hills under Tingridum.

The climate here was delightful, pleasantly

warm during the day, with a refreshing breeze blowing over the hills. The only drawback was the heavy fog which frequently rose from the river during the night, and did not disperse till about ten in the morning. It was worse than rain, penetrating everywhere; and condensing on the interior of the roof, it kept up a continual dripping from every blade of grass or pendent leaf.

A great protection against this mist were thick muslin mosquito curtains, made like a tent from the sloping sides of which the water ran off, and beneath which was to be found the only dry spot in the hut. The evenings were clear, star-lit, and cold—the average minimum temperature during the night being forty-four degrees.

When the mist did not trouble us in the early morning, the scenery was magnificent. On both sides the mist lay in the valleys like a sea of the softest wool, stretching away for miles, marking out each spur and ravine on the mountain sides like well defined shores. The peaks of the lower ranges stood up like little islands, while currents of air below dashed the mist against the steep out-running spurs, like mimic breakers against some bold headlands. The hills extended far away to the west, rising range upon range, purple and blue, till the sun, appearing above the bluff mass of the Surklang, lighted up the mountain sides with the most brilliant tints of orange and green, and changed the cold blue of the cloudy sea beneath, into all the varied and delicate tints of mother of pearl, while over all hung the canopy of clear lilac and gold of the morning sky. Such a scene requires a much more eloquent pen than mine to do justice to it, or even to convey any idea of its exceeding beauty.

> "I cannot paint
> The cataract, the tall rock,
> The mountain, and the deep and gloomy wood,
> Their colours and their forms."

CHAPTER XII.

SITE OF THE VILLAGE OF KHOLEL—VOUPILAL'S TOMB—ENGLOOM
—THE HEAD-MAN OF CHEPUI—SWEARING ETERNAL FRIEND-
SHIP — ARTISTIC JUDGMENT — DISTRIBUTION OF TROOPS—
MIDNIGHT PARLEYS—ATTEMPTED DECEPTION—LUSHAI WINE
APPRECIATED—VILLAGE LIFE.

CHAPTER XII.

ABOUT three miles south of No. 9. is the site
of the village of Kholel, in which lived
Voupilal, and where his tomb is still preserved.
Daidoo, Poiboi, and Kholel all acknowledged his
sway, and when on his death their inhabitants removed to Vanbong, they left the villages standing.
A fortnight before our arrival, however, they set
fire to them all, probably with a view to prevent
our finding any shelter in them on the march.

The path, as is the case along most of the ridges,
runs through very open jungle, till it reaches the
site of the village, a large bare gravelly spot, on
which stood, according to the Lushais, nearly a
thousand houses, but of which only a few
blackened uprights remain.

Old Kholel, most admirably situated beneath

N 2

one of the highest peaks of the range, where the
narrow ridge, widening as it gradually rises to
the hill, affords a site of half a mile in length,
and about three hundred yards in width, commanding a magnificent view of the Munipur,
Naga, and Jyntea hills on the North, and of the
Lushai and South Cachar hills on the East and
West.

Voupilal's house occupied a space forty yards
long by almost fifteen broad, as shewn still by a
few uprights and remnants of foundations, and at
the south end of its site is the tomb, a curious
structure consisting of a platform of rough flag-
stones and wood, about seventeen feet square and
three feet high. In the centre grows a young
banian tree, brought from below, which seems to
be flourishing in its elevated home. The whole
is surrounded by tall posts or trunks of small
trees, each crowned with the skulls of some
animal or animals slain in the chase; among
them are elephants, tigers, metuas, wild-boar,
deer, &c.

Of the metua, there are some thirty or forty
heads, round or near the tomb, and we also

found the head of a Munipuri pony, presented by the new rajah of that country to Voupilal a few years before.

There were two other smaller platforms surrounded with skulls close by, but for what purpose and with what intention they were erected, we were unable to find out.

On other posts drinking vessels, and wooden fetters used for securing captives, were hung. All are intended for the use of the deceased in the other world, where the animals whose heads surrounded his tomb will evermore be subject to him. No human skulls were discovered, although it is known that at least one Naga captive was slain at his death.

Standing about are curiously shaped posts branching out at the top, like the letter Y, and some ten feet high; these, we were told, were all sacrificial posts, on which metuas and other animals are sacrificed at the death of a chief.

The tomb is visible for miles around; a black speck, on a long bare yellow ridge, marking the spot where among the ruins of his villages, the mountain breezes for ever moaning over the sad deserted scene, rest the remains of the once powerful Lushai chieftain.

While at No. 9, we were frequently visited by large numbers of Lushais from Chepui and Tingridum, bringing in fowls, yams, and eggs for barter, the articles most coveted in exchange being cloth and salt.

A coolie, having no use for his money and being no doubt utterly tired of his monotonous Commissariat fare, gave one rupee for a fowl, which thenceforth was established by the Lushais as the standard price, though, of the actual value of the rupee they were entirely ignorant, appreciating more highly a few copper coins. A few sepoys who had a supply of the latter, took advantage of it to buy back at about a sixth of their value the rupees which the Lushais had previously received from the officers.

Out of the eight men who went into Cachar with the presents for Poïboi, one, Engloom by name, having no relations among the Lushais, and wishing ultimately to settle in Cachar, remained with us throughout the Campaign. This was the only man in our camp who knew any

thing at all of the country to the East, or the
position of the villages on our intended line of
march; and as we should have, from this point,
to trust a good deal to the information given us
by Lushais in the villages ahead, it was necessary, if possible, to avoid a collision with them.

On the 14th January, the headman of Chepui,
Tington, came in, in a scarlet cloak, a present
from the liberal British Government, attended by
several villagers. As they approached, they saw
some officers looking through telescopes at them,
and imagining these to be some deadly weapons,
they sat down to see what happened. As nothing
did happen, they rose and came on.

Whether from fear, or with the idea of keeping
up his dignity, the chief squatted with his back
to the camp at every hundred yards. " Whiles he
gaed, and whiles he sat," but at last he arrived
and had an interview with Mr. Edgar. He merely
said he was afraid of our destroying his village
and crops, and as usual he was told that, if he and
his people behaved properly, no injury would be
done to them.

Tington belongs to the Khengti family, which

the Lushai chiefs regard as equal in rank to their own. He is said to be a nephew of Vonolel; but he does not possess any power or influence at all commensurate with his high birth and pedigree.

We may dispose of him in this place by saying that he maintained friendly relations with us as long as our troops occupied the camp (No 10.) close to his village. He paid frequent visits to the officers in charge, and partook freely of the Commissariat rum, on which occasions he was often so overcome that he wept, and trying to fall on the shoulders of his hospitable enter-tainers, would swear eternal friendship in indis-tinct Lushai.

" One touch of nature makes the whole world kin," says a man who, even in his philosophy, never dreamt of Lushais; and Tington did but comport himself as I have often seen many civilised scions of aristocratic families nearer home doing on some festive occasion, vowing un-dying friendship for the chance companion of the hour; though I will do both the said scions and the Commissariat department the justice to add that, in the latter instances, that department has nothing to answer for.

As the roads in our rear were now passable for elephants, and as nothing, or next to nothing, was known of the route, or the people, or their temper, or the state of their defences, it was deemed advisable to bring up the artillery. Accordingly the two steel guns arrived on the 16th; the mortar it was found necessary to leave behind, and as things turned out it was never required.

In the afternoon of this day I had a visit from Santong, who wished to see my sketches. I showed him two little ones of Darpong and Rution Sing, which he recognised at once. He sat on the floor of the hut, looking at them, laughing occasionally, and gently repeating their names at intervals as if he expected to be answered. This he continued doing for about half an hour, and when asked to give back the sketches and portraits, could not be prevailed on to do so till he had called in a Sepoy, who was passing, to share his satisfaction.

In connection with this sketch of Darpong, the following incident illustrates the folly of jumping to conclusions. Several Lushais, having heard that I had a coloured sketch of that worthy gentle-

man, visited me, with the request that they might
be allowed to see my sketch-book, to which of
course I assented; and exhibited it to them. It
contained principally little pencil sketches, but at
last, on turning a page, a coloured picture appeared
to their delighted eyes. "Darpong," they all
cried at once; unfortunately they made a great
mistake, for it happened to be a landscape of an
up-country place of pilgrimage, named Hurdwar.

The 22nd arrived on the 13th at No. 9, and
on the 15th, went down and encamped at the
Tuivai, for the purpose of making the road up to
Chepui. About the same time, also, Major Moore
and Captain Heydayat Ali arrived, bringing their
Goorkha and Bhoolia coolies, the remnant who
had escaped the ravages of cholera at Chattuck.

Hitherto, the General had been deprived of
their services, and the Commissariat had often
been hard pushed to keep the supplies up to the
front; for while the Kholel sharp-shooters were
about, it was impossible to employ the elephants,
whose unwieldiness and unmanageableness, when
frightened, rendered them useless; but, on the
conclusion of the armistice, they were never idle.

With the exception of a strong guard at Mynadhur, the whole of the troops comprising the left
column, were at this time distributed at various
posts between No. 9 and Tipai Mukh.

On the 17th, leaving behind a guard of fifty
men of the 22nd under Lieutenant Gordon, the
General and staff, with Mr. Edgar and Col. Nuthall's
wing of the 44th, marched from Pachui, and descended to the Tuivai, here still a fine stream—
clear and cold, flowing between huge boulders,
past shingly reaches, and bubbling over pebbly
shallows, ever and anon widening out into still
pools, in the clear depths of which were reflected
the varied hues of the wooded hill-sides. A small
bamboo bridge had been thrown across at a spot
where a large stretch of shingle on the left bank
narrowed the stream considerably.

On the way down, a great many Lushais had
been observed collected in a joom opposite. A
few of them went down to the river, and the
General drew up his force on the shingle.

Darpong here arrived on the scene, and endeavoured to persuade the General to halt there
for the night, saying that Poiboi would parley in

the darkness. These midnight parleys seem to
be the usual custom among the Lushais, but it
was one to which the General did not feel bound
to conform, and the ascent was commenced up
the Lushai track.

After a quarter of an hour's climb the joom
in which the Lushais had been seen was reached.
About two hundred armed with muskets were
grouped in the centre, but immediately extended
in fighting order. They were all clad alike in
the usual grey sheet, with a small grey fillet
bound round the head, and a haversack across the
left shoulder.

The 44th, as they emerged on the joom, also
extended, forming a line facing the Lushais at
an interval of about a hundred and fifty yards.
The General, with his staff and Mr. Edgar,
occupying a spot half way between, directed
that Poiboi should come forward.

At some little distance stood a well-dressed
young fellow, and after a good deal of hurrying
about and preliminary consultations among the
Lushais, he came forward, accompanied by many
others. Mr. Edgar however, suspected, from

his manner, that he was not a chief, and Engloom, being called up, declared that he was not Poiboi, but a favourite companion of the latter.

On this the meeting broke up, it being explained to the Lushais that the General would have no further dealings either with Poiboi himself, or any other representative, till he had arrived at Chepui.

The Lushais again endeavoured, by threatening gestures, to prevent the advance, and it seemed as if Kholel was to be repeated here. However, the troops continued the ascent without taking any notice of the Lushais, and reached the village without further opposition.

After a climb from the Tuivai of two thousand two hundred feet up a steep and narrow rocky path, we crossed two or three pretty little mountain streams running over the moss and fern-covered rocks. These were bridged by Lushai structures; a couple of bamboos, or slender trees, supported on a few frail-looking uprights fixed in the crevices of the rocks below, affording a perilous passage to the booted invaders.

The artillery elephants were got up with much difficulty, and with fearful exertions on their own part, literally having to climb up some places. One practice they had, during any exertion, was peculiarly objectionable in the steep narrow track, I mean the habit of constantly dashing water on their bodies, wetting every one below with a muddy shower.

The column was halted near the village, where a few unfinished houses, intended to form a suburb of Chepui, were hired from the owners, and all the collected firewood purchased. The water supply was also very good, so on the whole we were more comfortable than we had been since the commencement of the campaign. The houses, being new, were free from the rats and fleas which disturbed our rest at the next village. The walls were made of bamboos, split and pressed out flat. The strips, thus obtained, having an average width of six inches, are interwoven horizontally and vertically, giving a chequered pattern to the walls, exceedingly pretty when new.

Engloom occupied a little hut in the centre,

and had managed to secure a large jar of the Lushai wine, which he was imbibing through reeds with several friendly Lushais. Some of the officers also tried it, and testified their approval by such frequent applications to the jar that Engloom took the opportunity of their superintending their camping arrangements to remove it to some place of concealment, and we saw it no more.

We had an opportunity of seeing a Lushai cooking operation performed on a fowl by Engloom. Squatting before a huge wood fire, he killed the bird by cutting its head off; and giving a few hurried plucks to some of the largest feathers, he flung the body into the midst of the flames. Snatching it out a second or two after, a few more feathers were plucked, and again it was thrown into the flames. These alternate burning and plucking operations were continued for about six or seven minutes, when the singed and blackened little mass was carried off to be devoured.

Not far off, another fowl was being roasted for the head-quarters' mess, but the *modus operandi* differed slightly from that of the Lu-shais. A long piece of wood, passed through the carefully plucked bird, was supported at each end by a small forked stick in front of the bright fire. A kitmutgar, sitting near, turned the piece of wood slowly round and round till the fowl was cooked.

In this camp we were protected from the cold winds and fog during the night and early morning, on one side by the high peak of Chepui, which rose one thousand two hundred feet above us, and on the other side by several wooded knolls, so that, though four hundred feet higher than at Pachui, the minimum temperature during the night was never below 50°.

The troops remained here till the 22nd January ; this delay being caused by the unwillingness of the villagers to point out any route except a very roundabout one by Tingridum ; and some of the troops actually commenced work upon it.

Colonel Roberts, feeling convinced that there must be a more direct road, was untiring in his endeavours to discover it, and at last success rewarded his efforts.

Previous to our arrival, all the women and children had been removed, and were concealed in some joom-houses on the hill sides, but before we left they were gradually returning and resuming their usual occupations. No efforts had been spared to inspire them with confidence, as it was very important to keep on good terms with the villages in the rear. Their sick were treated by our medical officers, and we heard that some of the wounded from Kholel were there. The villagers visited the camp daily, selling fowls and eggs. The latter were generally found to have been hard boiled.

Paper possessed great charms for them, and they would take newspapers up and walk quietly off with them, not being at all abashed if stopped and made to restore them; but when a paper was given them, they went proudly away with it sticking up from the back of their turbans (such as wore them) in the shape of a large fan or hood. Green and gold labels off pickle bottles, and brass labels off sardine boxes, found great favour as decorations for their hair knots.

In the meantime the survey party had visited

the highest peak of the Chepui hill, and clearing
it had erected a tall bamboo survey " mark." It
was about thirty feet high, and consisted of three
long poles planted in the ground and tied together
at the top in the form of a tripod. The top part
was closed in with bamboo matting, and a bamboo
basket surmounted the whole. These glittering
white marks can be seen when the sun is shining on
them for very long distances, and it is said were
supposed by the Lushais to be effigies of Her Most
Gracious Majesty, placed on their hill tops as
evidences of her greatness and the power of her
army to penetrate where it would.

CHAPTER XIII.

MORE SYMBOLIC WARNINGS—DESIGNS OF THE LUSHAI CHIEFS—
RECONNOITERING—DARPONG—ORDER OF MARCH—FIGHT WITH
THE LUSHAIS — SMALL BUT FORMIDABLE STOCKADE — THE
LUSHAIS TAKEN IN FLANK—CASUALTIES—NARROW ESCAPE
OF THE GENERAL.

CHAPTER XIII.

THE Western chiefs, Sukpilal and Khalkom, had not yet made their appearance, and Colonel Rattray, who was then commanding at Pachui, received orders to explore the roads in their direction, in order, if possible, to put pressure upon them.

According to the Lushais, Khalkom was ill and could not move. His illness, however, was never satisfactorily explained, and it was generally believed that he was wounded either at Kholel or Tipai Mukh.

As the time necessary for making roads could not be spared, the General determined to trust to the country paths from this point, taking on only the Artillery elephants. Those belonging to the Commissariat thenceforth worked only between

Tipai Mukh and Chepui; the supplies being taken on from the latter place by coolies.

On the 22nd January, the advance was continued along a very rocky path, the head-man, and two others from Tingridum, and three men from Chepui, accompanied it. The troops, who camped about three miles and a half from Chepui, on the banks of a little stream called Sairumlui, the next day climbed up to station No. 11, on the Gnaupa ridge, near the site of an old village called Bohmong.

Colonel Roberts, taking Engloom with him, went to explore the road ahead. The path divided into two shortly after leaving camp, one running along the ridge, the other along the east face of the hill towards Surklang. The latter was the route intended to be taken by the troops, and this was found blocked by a rude representation of men hanging on gallows; and a small red gourd, fixed in a tuft of grass, symbolised scalped heads for those who should go that way.

The path descended to a pretty little fordable stream called the Tuila, and crossed a steep spur of the Surklang to another stream, near which good camping ground was found.

On the return of the reconnoiterers, Mr. Edgar informed the Lushais with us that the Tuila route would be the one followed, and the head-man of Tingridum and Darpong were directed to go on and inform Poiboi that we should pass by his villages, but that, unless we were opposed, no harm would be done to them, and also that he must give up certain captives.

The Lushais earnestly begged that the General would reconsider his decision about the route, and take the Gnaupa one instead. This, they were told, was impossible, and they then asked that two young men of their number should be allowed to go on to the villages ahead.

The Lushais had expected us to cross the Lengteng by Gnaupa, and had fortified several strong points on it; and here they determined to make a great stand. The chiefs had declared their intention, if they succeeded in turning us back there, of harassing our retreat in every possible way, and not leaving off the pursuit till the troops reached the cultivated portion of

Cachar; while on the other hand, if we overcame all their opposition and crossed the Lengteng in spite of it, it was understood that our further advance on Chumfai would be unopposed.

In avoiding the steep and rocky passage of the Lengteng by that route, and choosing the easier one by Surklang and Muthilen, it was not the General's intention to avoid a collision with the Lushais; indeed it was desirable that a real trial of strength should take place between us and the whole force of the South-eastern tribes. Consequently when Darpong intimated that the real object of the two lads in wishing to leave us, was to recall the men stationed on Lengteng, they were allowed to go.

The interview between Mr. Edgar and the Lushais was carried on over our camp-fire after dinner, and loud and earnest were the sounds of the discussion which from time to time reached the ears of officers already retired to rest, one of whom, "little recking, if they would let him sleep on," of the great issue involved, and thinking they were some gossiping servants, requested them, in language more forcible than polite, to

cease chattering. No attention, however, was paid
to his modest request, and it was far into the night
when the Lushais at last left the camp. Shortly
afterwards two shots were heard by the advanced
picquet in the direction taken by the lads, but
nothing else occurred during the night.

In the morning, Darpong and the Tingridum
man also departed, and at eight o'clock the force
marched for the next camp; halting for a couple
of hours at the Tuila to allow the coolies to cook
and eat. As the supply of water at No. 11 had
been very limited, the General, Colonel Roberts,
and other officers, went on ahead to reconnoitre
the road in the afternoon. The path followed the
course of the ravine along its left bank. The ravine
was very narrow here, with densely wooded sides,
and the path, running over rocks and roots of
trees, in some places barely afforded a foothold,
while on the right below it was the rocky bed of a
mountain stream.

About a mile from camp the path again divided,
leading in one direction to the south over Muthilen
to the village of Kungnung, and in the other to
the east, up Surklang. The latter was the road

reconnoitred.   After climbing through some very
steep jooms, it ran along the south side of the
hill.   It was a tolerable road here, some three or
four feet wide, and evidently made in some parts
in others cut with daôs out of the hillside, the
best Lushai path we had yet met with.

After pursuing it for some time, and just as it
was so late as to necessitate a speedy return,
several large granaries were discovered in a joom,
and while these were being inspected, Darpong
and his companion appeared upon the scene.   On
questioning him as to his presence there, when
he was expected to have gone towards Poiboi's
village, which was in quite the opposite direction,
he said that the two shots we heard the night
before had been fired at the Lushais who left our
camp by people from Taikum, a large village a
mile or so further on the road, and that he had
been to inquire into the matter.   He also pointed
out to us Kungnung near the summit of Muthilen,
and said that both the villages were full of armed
men.   He then departed, promising to be in
camp next morning.

From the point where we met Darpong it was

easily seen that the onward route must be by Kungnung, as Chelam, Poiboi's village, was not visible over the high intervening hill. This being determined on, the reconnoitring party returned to their camp.

The night passed off quietly, and the troops marched again shortly after eight a.m. on the 25th. Darpong had come in and given the General to understand that an attack would be made on us in the ravine. Fifty men of the 44th went in advance, then the General and staff, and the wing of the 44th; sixty men of the 22nd being left as a guard for the Artillery and coolies, for whose safety all felt very anxious.

Such was the order of march for the small force with him, and considering the precipitous nature of the hill-sides, which completely commanded the narrow rocky stream, the General felt that he could not search the banks as he went along.

About half a mile from camp, however, as the advanced guard were climbing over a steep rocky part of the path, the first shots were exchanged, and as if by magic along the whole line and in

front, the gloom of the forest was lighted up by a
myriad of flashes, and bullets and slugs fell
around us,

> " As on a July day,
> The thunder shower falls pattering on the way."

At the first discharge the General's orderly
was shot dead from the the right bank, and almost
immediately the General himself was wounded in
the left arm and hand by a Lushai on the left
bank, not eight yards off.

The Sepoys replied well, and Captain Robertson's advanced guard extended as they reached
the rocky ground on the left flank, while the rest
of the 44th, under Colonel Nuthall and Captain
Lightfoot, flinging down their packs and great-
coats, dived into the rocky stream, and meeting
the enemy in their own jungle, almost hand to
hand, drove them up the hill before them, scatter-
ing them most effectually. Thirteen Lushais
fell almost in one spot in the stream, those who
were not dead being despatched without mercy.

One man was trying to escape up the face of
a piece of rock over which some water trickled
into a pool below. The slippery rock hindered

him, and ere he could mount it a Goorkha had overtaken him and cut him down with his kookrie. He fell on his face in the pool, looking painfully like a woman, as he lay there with his smooth cheek and neatly braided hair and knot.

The General's wounds having been speedily bound up, he was enabled shortly to overtake the troops again.

At the very commencement of the firing, a note was sent by Mr. Edgar from the camp, telling the General that he had forced Darpong to state what he knew about the intended attack. His statement was, that the Lushais meant to avoid the troops, but to attack the coolies and artillery elephants. Two of Mr. Edgar's Cachari coolies were wounded at the outset, and this dispiriting the others, that gentleman determined· to remain with them. Captain Thompson also remained behind.

Some of the Lushais managed to slip past the column, and attacked the rear, and as we climbed the hill in pursuit of the Lushais, we could hear the firing below.

On collecting the scattered columns, the advance followed the Kungnung path through some open jooms, from which we could see the Lushais running wildly about on the spurs and ridges above, apparently endeavouring to collect for a stand at the village.

At length the path ran along the face of a huge precipice, and was commanded for a long distance by a small stockade, constructed at the most difficult part of the road, where a few resolute men might have stopped the advance of an army, while a few rocks detached from above would have inflicted heavy loss on the troops passing beneath, as escape would have been impossible. At this very point, a fortnight later, a small hill pony, belonging to an officer, slipped and went over the path, and falling three hundeed feet, was killed at once.

The rapidity with which the advance had been conducted, had left the Lushais no time to defend this stockade; but passing onwards, the path suddenly emerged on a joom, above which, and on the high crest of another precipitous ridge, was another long stockade. The foremost Sepoy, on showing himself at the edge of the joom, was at once saluted with a shot, which fortunately missed him. It was found useless to take this stockade with a rush, owing to the nature of the ground, and so two parties of the 44th, under Capts. Robertson and Lightfoot, skirmished round to their right, taking advantage of some long grass jungle which concealed them from the defenders of the stockade, who kept up a steady fire on the road, expecting to see the troops appear every moment.

The rest of the force had been halted under shelter of the bank, till the result of the flank movement should be apparent. This manœuvre was most successfully executed, and great must have been the surprise of the Lushais, while keeping their attention and fire directed on the path in front, to find themselves suddenly taken in flank. They fled, scarcely exchanging a shot with their unexpected assailants; and, when the troops advanced through the stockade to the village, a couple of hundred yards beyond, not a Lushai was visible, all having vanished in the forest and down the hill-side.

The troops at once occupied the village. The fires were found burning in the houses, domestic articles were lying about as if abandoned in haste; and a few dogs, cowering in corners, testified to the unpreparedness of the Lushais for this result of their attack. In some houses were picked up white skirts, which had been distributed to some of the people who had visited us at Chepui.

The artillery elephants could not be got up to the village that evening, being unable to climb the latter part of the track, and so encamped below the stockade. The coolies, with the whole of the baggage, arrived in camp by seven P.M.

Owing to the excellent arrangements made for the protection of the elephants and coolies by Major Moore, in charge of the Coolie Corps, Captain Udwy, 44th, commanding the rear-guard, and Lieutenant Hall, 22nd, commanding the supports, the casualties were less than might have been expected, only one coolie being killed, while two were wounded severely, and one slightly. The other casualties for the day were as follows: killed—two non-commissioned officers and one man of the 44th; wounded Artillery, two severely; 44th, one severely; Police, one severely.

General Bourchier's wounds were re-examined as soon as the medical officers arrived at Kungnung. He had a very narrow escape. He himself at first thought that he was wounded in the left hand only, and it was not till he took off his coat that a hole was discovered under and behind his left elbow; and a wound which was found in his fore-arm at once accounted for the pain he felt there. Fortunately for the Left Column, the General's wounds, though painful, did not disable him, excepting so far as they neccessitated a sling for a short time.

CHAPTER XIV.

COUNCIL OF THE CHIEFS—OUR WEAK POINT—KUNGNUNG—THE
LENGTENG RANGE—ADVANCE OF THE TROOPS—A STRONG
STOCKADE—A DETOUR—ARTILLERY PRACTICE—EFFECT OF
SHELLS—STRIKING SCENE—A CURIOUS GRAVE.

CHAPTER XIV.

THERE must have been some great defect in the tactics of the Lushais to account for their signal defeat. It appears that the very night before, a great council of all the chiefs of the families of Vonolel and Lalpoong had been held in the village of Kungnung; and then Poiboi had been induced to throw in his lot finally against us.

At this meeting, the course of action to be pursued against us on the following day was decided on. One party was to divert the attention of the main force, while the other, stealing down the ravine, would, when the troops were considered far enough advanced, attack the coolies, who, they imagined, would be unprotected. They thus hoped, by killing a number of the coolies, so to demoralise the rest that, being deprived of our

means of transport, we should be compelled to
retire; this idea, as we have seen, was better
conceived than carried out.

Mr. Edgar imagines that this scheme originated
with the head man of Tingridum, who had stated
truly that our weak point was the long line of
coolies following the main body. Darpong advised Mr. Edgar of this plan of operations of the
Lushais before the firing commenced, probably
out of spite for him of Tingridum, with whom he
had a quarrel, carefully fostered by the authorities.

The principal causes of the utter failure on the
part of the Lushais, I believe to be these. In the
first place they were not sure which of the two
routes we would take, though they probably inclined to the one reconnoitred the day before, and
consequently were afraid to concentrate their forces
on either. Secondly, the hour fixed for marching
was earlier than usual, and it is probable that
the party the advanced guard fell in with was the
one intended to watch the coolies. They had not
had time to finish their ambuscading arrangements
before we met, and scattered them so completely
that only a few were able to carry out their in-

structions, while the advance on Kungnung was so rapid that the enemy were unable to collect in sufficient force to make an effectual resistance at the stockades.

From accounts afterwards received by Mr. Edgar, it seems probable that the Lushai loss in killed and wounded was over sixty.

The utter discomfiture of the Lushais was evident from the fact of their leaving so many of their dead in the ravine, having only time to cut off and carry away the heads of two of these; and even when next day a party was sent down to burn the dead bodies, and to recover some great-coats, &c., which had been overlooked, the former were found lying as they had been left, no attempt apparently having been made by their friends to remove them.

Among the slain were two head men, one of whom was Poiboi's chief adviser. We got seven muskets, and in one of their havresacks was found some of our own smooth-bore ammunition, apparently identifying the owner with one of the raiders of 1871, at Monirkhal or Nudigram.

Kungnung contained twenty-two houses situated on the slope of a peak five thousand feet in height, just south of which Muthilen rises to a height of nearly six thousand feet. The approach on all sides is very difficult, the slopes of the hill being exceedingly precipitous and broken by huge masses of rock.

The hills south and east of this range assume quite a different character from those to the north-west and west, being much more rocky, and consequently less jungly; long grass and bracken taking the place of the irritating undergrowth of thorny jungle previously met with.

Surklang is an immense mass of peaks tossed about in wild confusion, the rocks dropping out in irregular strata, now horizontal, now following the general inclination of the spurs ; and further to the east the Lengteng range presents the appearance of a large buttressed wall, its top being square and level for the greater part of its length, and the west face precipitous—a few narrow spurs giving the idea of buttresses, and the almost perfectly horizontal rocky strata the idea of courses of masonry ; a few trees appear near the summit.

From Kungnung we could see nearly every station in our rear as far as No. 6 ; and as the mantle of night descended on the hills, the gleaming fires appearing one by one on the successive ridges marked the position of each camp.

In order to follow up the successes of the 25th, the General issued instructions to Colonel Roberts to take a force, consisting of two steel guns of the Mountain Battery, and a hundred men from the 22nd and 45th regiments, and burn the village of Taikum on the 26th.

As already stated, the Artillery could not get into camp on the 25th, so the force for the Taikum Expedition was delayed in starting till twelve noon. The path to Taikum lay due east, descending for about a mile and a half till it reached the head of the stream just below the saddle connecting Surklang and Muthilen, whence ascending again it joined the path reconnoitred on the 24th.

From this reconnaissance it was evident that the guns would never reach Taikum that day, if carried on elephants ; consequently, the General decided that they should be carried by coolies.

Sixteen men were told off for each gun, viz., six for the gun itself, which weighed a hundred and fifty pounds, six for the carriage, and two for each wheel, besides four for the ammunition boxes, each box containing nine rounds.

On arriving at the joom in which we had before discovered the granaries, we found all but two had been burnt. These two had been pulled down, but the grain had not been removed.

Proceeding onwards some little distance, the road suddenly turned and ran round the re-entering angle between two large spurs. Across this valley, about a mile off, we perceived a strong stockade, built across the road, command-ing it thoroughly. A steep rocky ravine ran up on its right flank, and a large number of the enemy were collected at that point.

If the troops could have been got nearer, Colonel Roberts would have advanced the infantry under cover of the artillery. The nature of the ground did not allow of this, except at the risk of heavy loss. So a detour was made, entailing a long and weary drag up and down steep spurs, at one time attaining the height of six thousand feet, till at last we struck the road again about a mile beyond the stockade.

The Lushais had been watching our movements from various points, and finding their stockade turned, they retired at once to their village. Soon after we started from the camp Mr. Edgar discovered that the head-man of Tingridum had disappeared, and it was supposed had gone in the direction of Taikum.

Notice of this was sent to Colonel Roberts. We soon, however, met the supposed fugitive near the stockade, accompanied by three of the villagers, waving their hands about to show they were unarmed. The head-man said he had gone so far to get rice for Darpong, and showed us a little in his hand as proof; but as there was plenty at Kungnung, and the amount he had with him was scarcely sufficient for one meal, this was an evident falsehood.

As soon as the villagers discovered that we intended to go on to their village, they tried to get away. They were stopped, however, and made to accompany the force.

In consequence of the detour and the frequent

delays to enable the guns to keep up with the troops, it was five o'clock when, on turning a corner, we came in sight of Taikum. This village is situated on the summit of a small hill, contains about two hundred houses, and is surrounded by a strong palisado. It was full of men.

We were then distant twelve hundred yards from it, and commanded the village thoroughly, a small level piece of ground on the right of the road affording ample space for bringing the guns into action, which was accordingly done. The Lushais had evidently become aware of our approach, and collected all their force in a large open space at the top of the village to watch our movement.

The three villagers squatted near the guns to see what would happen to their friends and houses. The practice was excellent. At the first there was a movement among the enemy, as if they were going to run away, but nothing immediately following they stood firm. The Sepoys also, not knowing the time necessary for the flight of the projectiles, gave vent to a few murmurs of disappointment, which were speedily changed to cries of delight, as the puff of smoke just over the village, followed by the report, announced the bursting of the shell.

The fuze having been set for a longer range, the villagers could not have seen it burst, as they still remained where they were. To the Lushais with us, it appeared as if it had gone on to the hill across the valley, "a day's journey off," as they wonderingly said to each other.

The second gun was beautifully laid, and the shell burst in the very centre of the group of men, who seemed completely paralyzed at first, but soon commenced to run down the narrow streets. A few appeared to be incapable of motion, but others returned to carry them off.

In the meantime Colonel Roberts, directing Captain Blackwood to fire two more rounds at the retreating foe, advanced rapidly with the infantry, and as the latter entered the village from one side, the former evacuated it on the other, firing only two shots, without effect, as they disappeared down the hill sides. It was nearly six o'clock then, and it was useless to pursue them; so the village was set fire to at once.

A few of the Goorkas had secured some pigs, which, being too big to be 'carried whole, were killed with a knock on the head, and the shoulders and the hind-quarters were sliced off with two or three strokes of their handy kookries. Then all the troops having fallen in again, the return march commenced.

As we gained the knoll from which the guns had been fired, and looked back, the scene was very striking. Behind a huge misty mountain the calm moon rose bright and clear in the pale green sky, illumining the far off ranges, while nearer, the red flames and smoke, and sparks, swept away to the left by the evening breeze, lighted up the foreground with a ruddy glow, to which intensity was added by the deep black mass of huge forest which partially hid Taikum from our gaze; while, below in the wide slip between us and the village, a small stream flowed, reflecting on its surface the red glare of the flames.

Fortunate was it that we had the moon to guide our returning steps over the weary five miles that lay before us, as even with its assistance it was nearly eleven P.M., before we reached the camp, after a rather hard day's work.

Beacon signals had informed the neighbouring villages of the intended attack on us on the 25th, and the inhabitants of Chepui and Tingridum and Kholel had again fled into the jungles; but the judicious measures taken by the officers commanding at Chepui and Tuibum, succeeded in restoring confidence and they soon returned.

In consequence of the Tingridum head-man having left the camp without leave on the 2nd, he was fined one hundred and thirty baskets of rice, a pig, and a goat. A man was sent on the 27th to Tingridum, to tell the villagers to deliver these articles to the officers at Chepui, and this was done at once.

Darpong was also sent on to Poiboi, to tell him that, as he had attacked us on the 25th, the General had altered the terms on which he would consent to receive him, and that, in addition to giving up his captives, he must pay a fine of rice, metuas, pigs, goats, and fowls.

On the 27th a party escorted a large body of coolies to the jooms near Taikum, and brought in all the grain we had seen ·in the two store-houses there. A large quantity of rice, beans, yams, &c., in big baskets was also discovered in a cave near Kungnung; and the supply thus obtained assisted the Commissariat considerably, and for a couple of days many of the coolies were employed in husking the rice in the village.

The troops had been distributed in the various houses, a large house at the bottom of the village being used as the quarter-guard. This had been the head-man's house, apparently, and when we first arrived there we saw a curious grave outside.

This grave consisted of a tall post set up over a mound, enclosed with rough stones, and covered with a metua's head, through which a small stick was passed, carrying a goat's head, and a large coronet of cane-work, in which countless feathers of all sorts and colours were fixed. Below the metua's head was a similar coronet, but smaller, from which strings of smaller skulls, dogs', monkeys', &c., were suspended round the post; while outside the stones towered two tall bamboos, having at their ends, small cane circles, bearing little bamboo strips, which swinging about in the wind make a doleful rattling sound.

The General had a hut constructed for himself and Staff above the village. The houses would not have been uncomfortable dwellings, but for the rats which swarmed at nights, scampering over our faces or falling from the roof. The only way to ensure ourselves against these little annoyances was to put up musquito curtains, fastening them down securely at the sides and ends.

CHAPTER XV.

TELEGRAM FROM CACHAR—RESCUE OF MARY WINCHESTER—
FIGHT OF LUSHAIS AND CLASSIS — ESCAPE OF A LUSHAI
PRISONER—A DISTURBER OF THE CAMP—TOUCHING SCENE—
THE SAIVAR—POIBOI'S STRONGHOLD—A CURIOUS HUNT—
ALARM OF FIRE—A THOUGHTFUL BOY.

CHAPTER XV.

ON the 28th a telegram was received from Cachar, stating that Sukpilal's muntri Rowa, had arrived at Jhalnachara, with the Khansaman's wife and a Cachari, who had been taken prisoners at Alexandrapur.

The officiating Deputy Commissioner, Mr. McWilliam, also telegraphed that Sukpilal had Mary Winchester, and said, as soon as he got a boat, he would send her into Cachar. This intelligence put everybody in a great state of excitement; the child was rescued and would be restored to her friends, through the officer commanding the left column.

A little consideration, however, showed that it was highly probable that this information was not to be relied on. The Syloos, it was known, had the child, and as the other column was operating against them, it was hardly likely they would throw away their best card, when by keeping it they might hope to secure favourable terms for themselves when the proper time for playing it arrived.

And so it proved. Mary Winchester was given up to the other column. This news was telegraphed by General Brownlow, and was received on the 29th at Kungnung.

During the next two days, the Lushais came in, bringing in metuas, &c., in payment of the indemnity inflicted on Poiboi for his share in the attack on the 25th.

On the 31st, Dambhung, head-man of Taikum, and the Chief of Poiboi's ministers, arrived in camp, bringing letters from General Nuthall, in which he stated that there was much sickness among the Munipur contingent, and they had moreover a defective Commissariat.

Dambhung said that he was at Chibu during the fighting on the 25th and 26th, and was much surprised on his return to find that his village had been destroyed from off the face of the earth.

It is not improbable that he was occupied with some Lushai troops watching the contingent, to prevent, if possible, the latter assisting us when we were attacked. He also said that Poiboi had striven hard, at the Council held at Kungnung on the 24th, to induce his relatives to submit, but in vain.

The supply of water was not very good at this village. There were two little springs, both fully a quarter of a mile from the camp, and with every arrangement of wells, but they could not be made to yield a sufficient supply, to prevent the coolies and Sepoys stirring the water up and making it muddy, when they filled their vessels.

On the 31st, as one of our survey classis (men employed to carry instruments, &c.,) was returning with two brass vessels full of water in each hand, he met two Lushais who had passed the night in camp, on the narrow pathway. A scuffle ensued, and one of the Lushais wounded the classi severely with his daô on the forehead, just missing his eye, but penetrating the skull, and also on the arm. The other then seized the classi's red turban and his water-pots, and the two immediately made off.

The classis, being principally Hindus, and possessing strong caste prejudices, had frequently driven away with much harshness any Lushai who ignorantly approached too close to their cooking-pot or fire-place, while preparing their food. It is not unlikely, therefore, that this lordly invader had endeavoured to make the Lushais get out of his way, and that the latter had resented this insult in the usual manner with the daô.

This was the explanation tendered by an officer of great experience among the natives, and though another worthy officer disposed of this argument entirely to his own satisfaction by the simple and laconic reply of " Bosh," I cannot help thinking that there was a good deal of probability, to say the least, in it.

The Lushai, a fine spirited-looking youth, returned to Kungnung with a metua in the afternoon, was recognised, admitted at once that he had done the deed, and was apparently surprised to find himself tied up as a prisoner, remarking that when Poiboi heard how he had been treated it would be bad for us.

I made a sketch of him as he sat bound outside the guard-room, evidently objecting to this enforced " sitting for his portrait." His whole attitude, and the vigilant look in his eyes, reminded me strongly of some noble wild animal held captive, eagerly watching for the slightest opportunity of escape ; and such an opportunity presented itself to him, or rather he made it for himself the very next day, when, the troops having left Kungnung, his Goorkha guard was exchanged for one of Sappers and Miners, who were left behind to occupy the place.

The Goorkhas, in the Jynteah and Cossyah Hill wars, had learnt, from sad experience, how easily a Hillman will escape if not carefully bound and watched, and had paid no attention to Simlam's signs that he was too tightly tied. These however he repeated to the less experienced and more tender-hearted Sappers, and they loosed his bonds slightly.

He then signed for some covering, and they put a rug over his shoulders.

Suddenly, taking advantage of a moment when the sentry had relaxed his vigilance, this Lushai

Davenport Brother, flinging off rug and bonds together, and clearing the guard-house at a bound, disappeared into the jungle, before his discomfited guards could recover from their astonishment, to offer any opposition. He was to have been sent to Cachar, to be imprisoned there. His escape, however, probably saved us from a great deal of " political complications."

On the 1st February, the General and staff with Mr. Edgar, and the advanced detachments of the 22nd and 44th regiments, marched out of Kungnung along the western face of Muthilen. The path was narrow, and on a steep hillside, broken here and there by rocks and landslips.

At length, after a weary toil under a hot sun, a little stream was reached where the force waited for a short time, refreshing themselves with the clear cold water, while a small party went on to find, if possible, a better camping ground ahead. This they did, and at five P.M. the troops reached the banks of a swiftly running stream, with a gravelly bed, the water cold as if iced.

Lofty hills rose on all sides; and the elevation of the site was about five thousand two hundred feet. The atmosphere was very damp and cold, the thermometer going down during the night to thirty-nine degrees. The gloom of the virgin forest seemed never to have been penetrated by the sun's rays.

The huge forest trees were festooned with moss and creepers, and a curious bamboo was found here, which we saw nowhere else; each joint having a ring of thorns round it, and the joints seldom more than eight inches apart.

In cutting some of these to build our huts, we found enclosed between the joints of a bamboo, four little bats, alive. How they came there, how long they had been there, and how being there they would, without our assistance, ever have got out, I leave to be explained by those who know all about the curious stories of toads found in coal, for I confess myself unable to solve the mystery. The joints of the bamboo certainly seemed perfectly air-tight, for there was no perceptible opening.

We had only time to construct hasty cantos of boughs and leaves; and we soon discovered the disadvantages of attaching the framework of the maichâns to that of the walls of the canto, as the slightest movement on the part of any one sleeper communicated a vibration to the whole structure that soon aroused all the other occupants.

I awoke in the middle of the night with a sensation of cold about my head, and hearing an unusual noise close to my ear. I looked up, and perceived by the light of the many camp-fires struggling through the mist, in which the giant moss-grown trunks loomed vast and weird, that a large gap had been made in the leafy wall, and putting out my hand it came in contact with a pony's head. I gave it a blow, and it went away, but shortly afterwards I heard sounds the reverse of blessing proceeding from a hut near.

In the morning we found that the offender, who had disturbed our repose, was an officer's pony, which had got loose, and gone round the camp, devouring each hut in turn, till the sleeper within was aroused and drove it away.

A heavy dew fell in the morning, and very glad everyone was to get some hot tea and depart.

Here we received the news of Simlam's escape.

About nine a.m., the force commenced the onward march for Chelam, Poiboi's chief village,
which we expected to reach that evening. The
march was pleasant enough for the first four
or five miles, lying along the east face of Lengteng, through light forest, with grass and
fern undergrowth. There were a great many
orchids on the trees, but not in bloom; and in
one place we saw a young fir springing up
through the grass.

The road passed over several precipices, down
which dashed little mountain streams; at one
of the most romantic of these, we were overtaken by Darpong, and a large number of
Lushais bringing the metuas and elephant tusks.

Among them came Bhoma, a Kholel man,
with a captive Naga woman, whom he had taken
from Munipur in 1869. A most touching scene
ensued. Mr. Edgar, through his interpreter,
informed her, in an affecting speech, that she
might consider herself free to return with her
liberators to the land of her birth.

To the surprise of everyone, however, instead
of expressing joy, she took her pipe out of her

mouth, burst into a torrent of tears, and falling
on Bhoma's shoulder, declared, in broken language, that he had ever been kind to her, and,
like Mrs. Micawber, that " she could never,
never desert him." Unlike Mr. Micawber, poor
Bhoma could not reply, " I am not aware, my
love, that anyone wishes you to do so," for not
only was a stony-hearted Political wishing it,
but apparently urging her to do so. However,
her distress was evidently real, and though neither young nor pretty, the sight of her tears
moved even that gentleman at last, and he declared, in another feeling address, that he would
not constitute himself the Lord Penzance of the
Lushais, nor come between her and the object
of her elderly affections. This faithful one, then
relieved from her suspense, walking hand in
hand with her nearly lost Lushai lord, followed
us on to Chelam.

During our march, we crossed, about two p.m.,
a fine stream called the Saivar, at an elevation
of three thousand seven hundred feet, and
after a short ascent came upon a large open
park-like plain, still covered with the stubble of

recent cultivation. From this the ascent was very steep through old jooms to the hill above, on the other side of which was Chelam, at an elevation of five thousand eight hundred feet.

At length, after a severe climb, in rounding a spur, we came in full view of Poiboi's stronghold. It was a large village.

Poiboi's own house stood high above the others, which rose in tiers on each side of broad streets, stretching away down the slopes of the hill in all directions. There were about two hundred houses, the whole enclosed in a stiff timber stockade.

Beyond this village rose two other peaks, on which stood two smaller villages, also stockaded, and containing between them some three hundred houses.

No Lushais being seen, the troops marched into the principal village. Near the gate was a timber platform, with the usual posts capped with skulls; among them, on a lofty pole, one human skull, marking the grave of a departed warrior; others were scattered along the paths between the three villages.

These had not long been deserted, as the fires were still smouldering, and trays, half filled with grain, were lying about. The houses were speedily told off to the different corps, and every-one commenced his arrangements for the night.

In the middle of these, we suddenly heard great shouts and uproar and much squeaking; and running out to see what was the matter, we beheld a most ridiculous sight. The Kookie and other Hill coolies, having got rid of their loads, had discovered a few pigs trying to hide away under some of the houses in a by-street, and in hunting these they succeeded in unearthing a great many more.

Emerging from under the houses, and hurrying down the steep and narrow street, went the pigs, and after them, in full cry, armed with every variety of weapon, sticks, daôs, kookries, rushed the coolies pell-mell; tumbling over each other in their eagerness, and whacking at each unfortu-nate porker as it was overtaken.

Some were killed at once; others, generally prize-sows, whose forms were not adapted to feats of agility, being quickly overtaken, had their four feet tied together despite their remonstrances, and bamboos being passed between their legs, they were carried off to be killed and cut up at leisure.

Great was the consumption of frizzled pork that night; some of it, as we shall see, being wasted in the way described by Charles Lamb as leading to the discovery of the excellence of that viand when so cooked.

This little excitement was soon over; and we again returned to our abodes. My chief, two officers of the 22nd, and myself occupied one of the town halls, a fine commodious, though slightly airy building, with an immense fireplace, in which the ashes were still smouldering. This fireplace was in the centre of the room, and sunk about a foot below the general level of the floor, thus affording many comfortable sittings all round the fire. The principal drawback was the unsound state of the floor, which at one time caused the sudden disappearance from our gaze of a kitmutgar with part of the dinner, which we could ill-afford to lose; however, we did very well, and about ten P.M. turned in, very glad, after a rather hard day's work, to get to rest.

R

We had not been to sleep an hour before the alarm of fire was given, and starting up we found that the lowest houses in one of the streets were in flames; and the wind blowing upwards, great fears were entertained as to the probable destruction of the whole village. The houses were dry and closely packed, and a single spark, or bit of smouldering tinder, carried by the breeze into the thatch, was sufficient to set a house on fire at once.

The only thing to be done was to try to stay the progress of the fire by pulling down and removing, as far as possible, the most inflammable portions, such as the thatch, matting, &c., of the houses nearest the fire. Considerable exertions were made by all, and eventually proved successful, aided by a fortunate change in the direction of the wind, which carried the sparks harmlessly down the hill-side. Then, having covered the smouldering mass with earth, and leaving some Sepoys to see that the fire did not break out afresh, everyone went back to his quarters.

Among the officers attached to the Column, there was one who was a great enthusiast for

colours, and possessed great appreciation of
effects. Watching the fire, lighting up with its
ruddy glare the sky, the village, and the forms
of men rushing to and fro, he exclaimed, "Magnificent! magnificent! put it all in gamboge!"
to which a grinning friend of his, passing at the
moment, rejoined, "If you would put it all out
with gamboge, it would be more to the purpose
just now."

I found that my boy, with a forethought not
often met with in natives, had refrained from
running to see the fire, and had packed up everything ready for an instant move, as he had done
once before on the first alarm in the attack on
Tipai Mukh, as if he expected that, the moment
the Lushais appeared, we should all get into boats
and sail gaily away.

On this occasion his prudence involved some
delay in getting to bed again, as all the bedding
had to be unrolled and re-arranged. It was probable that the fire was caused by some of the
Kookies roasting their pork; and indeed, even
while the fire was raging, and it was a toss up
whether the whole village did not go, I saw some

coolies, sitting under the eaves of a house, cooking over a big fire, and the flames were within an inch of the dry thatch when I perceived them, fortunately.

It was thought at first that this conflagration was the work of an incendiary; but that was most unlikely, as Poiboi had consented to our occupying the village provided no damage was done to it.

Of the two hundred houses in the village, only twenty-five, and one of the town-halls, were burnt or destroyed, as before related.

Poiboi's house was similar to the one described in the Chapter on the Lushais; the gable end was completely covered with skulls, among which was the finest pair of metua's horns we saw anywhere, as well as some magnificent specimens of sambar's antlers.

The house itself was in rather a ruinous state, and being built on sloping ground, the front verandah was raised about twelve feet, and the sloping ramp of logs up to it decidedly dangerous. Rice, Indian corn, yams, herbs, &c., gourds of pig's lard, and large clay vessels of wine, were found in most of the houses.

CHAPTER XVI.

THE TROOPS ENCAMPED—LALBOORA'S GATE—A VISIT TO NATIVE
VILLAGERS—TELESCOPES—DIFFICULTY OF OBTAINING PHOTO-
GRAPHS—CAPTIVES PLACED UNDER OUR PROTECTION—THE
MUNIPUR CONTINGENT — POIBOI'S VACILLATION — LUSHAI
FORTIFICATIONS—A LUSHAI TODTLEBEN.

CHAPTER XVI.

HAVING so narrowly escaped this danger from fire, and the loss of property which must have followed it, if it had not been got under, and dreading a recurrence of the evil, the General determined to leave the village and to encamp in the open, wherever a good supply of water could be found. A small reconnoitring party, therefore, started early in the morning, and at last found very good camping ground, on the slopes of the hill, about a mile and a half from the village we had occupied, with a very fair spring of water.

The ground for each corps was allotted to it, and soon huts were being constructed or tarpaulins rigged up. To the right and left of the camp stretched the range, rising in the rear to a height of two hundred feet, bleak and rugged. Bare jooms covered with long grass and the stubble of old crops, huge trunks of felled trees lying about in all directions, blackened stumps, and a few tall trees which had escaped the fire and the daô, still standing up out of the stubble—these were the immediate surroundings of the camp.

To the south and east, the view on a fine day is magnificent, an endless sea of hills stretching away as far as the eye can see, lighted up by a thousand soft and delicate tints ; and nearly due south, distant some fourteen miles as the crow flies, are Dilklang and Murklang, towering above their fellows like two giant warders, and guarding the entrance to Lalboora's country. To this pass we gave the name of Lalboora's Gate.

Between this gate and Chelam lie many deep valleys and high ranges, the sides of which are broken by innumerable gloomy gorges and dark ravines. Very dreary and threatening does this country look on a stormy day, and very cold was our camp at night, the thermometer frequently going down as low as 33 degrees, while the ground about our huts, and the waterproof sheets above them, were white with hoar-frost in the mornings.

Strong winds swept up from the deep valley beneath, carrying off our fires in great swirls of sparks, and driving the pungent wood-smoke into our eyes with a force and painfulness that caused hasty flight from our log seats in all directions.

To remedy this, we built semi-circular screens of boughs and grass, about six feet high, round the front of the huts, leaving only a small passage at each end, and after that we could sit round the fire with much more comfort.

After we left the village, some of the men came back to it; but most of them, with their women and children, remained in the jungles north of the Tuivai stream. From the hill behind the camp we could see, in the evening, the smoke of their fires curling up through the trees on the hill side. They feared to return, as Poiboi was still so undecided, and could not be induced to go in personally to make terms for himself, fearing a similar fate to that of Lalchokla in 1844.

In a little village, however, about four miles from our camp, and on the same range, the people were all living and pursuing their usual occupations. We paid them a visit one day; Captain Cookesley, R.A., taking his camera and tent for photographing.

The villagers were very friendly; men, women, and children flocked about to see what we had to show them. Binoculars, eye-glasses, telescopes, watches, and the camera were all, in turn, the subject of wonder and delight to the simple savages.

In this village we saw a house, in front of which were five tall posts bearing rude representations of hornbills, thoroughly conventional, the only part in which there was any resemblance being the beak. Above each dangled a circlet of bamboo pendent. For what reason these were placed there we were unable to discover, having, unfortunately, no interpreter with us.

The camera was set up and focussed in the house, and then the Lushais were allowed to file behind it, looking through as they passed, and great was their wonder and delight when they saw the house and their friends about it turned upside down.

Telescopes pleased them very much. Mr. Burland told me that, in his previous expedition with Mr. Edgar, he had shown them his telescope, and making them first look through the eye-piece, said, " When I want to shoot a man, I look through this end, and bring him very close." Then reversing it for them, he added, " But when I see a man wishes to shoot me, I look through it this way, and he is sent so far away that he cannot touch me;" and they believed this. Seeing so many new and wonderful things they could not understand, this did not appear altogether incredible, as they actually saw the difference in the appearance of objects as seen through each end of the telescope.

Revolvers excited their highest admiration, and many would have given almost all they had to become the possessor of one.

Cookesley found it impossible to get figures in his pictures. The noble savage would stand motionless for half-an-hour while the plate was being prepared, but just as the cap was removed, he would calmly stroll right across the picture, and we could not explain to them what they were to do.

We bought some fowls and eggs, which one of their number carried for us, and we returned to camp.

In exploring the village nearest our camp, we found a grave newly made, and remains of a metua, hastily slain, lying near, the head as usual having been placed above. Probably this was the burial-place of some warrior who had died of his wounds, received on the 25th, and whose funereal ceremonies they had only just been able to perform before " the foe and the stranger should tread o'er his head."

In front of the Muntri's house was a large headless monkey stuffed, and sitting on the doorway, his legs sticking out straight before him; altogether a most ludicrous looking object. This village was more full of fleas than I could have believed any place to be. Even in the middle of the street, they were to be found as plentiful as in the house.

I sat down in the street for a few minutes to take a sketch, and I found on rising that they were even in possession of my innermost pockets, and added warmth to the colour of my light brown coat.

An old woman, a captive, was found in Chelam and placed under our protection, to be conveyed to Cachar, and on the 7th February a little girl about four years old was brought into camp. She was said to have been brought from the Howlongs by Poiboi or Laboora. Her own account was that she had been taken off from a garden, and she spoke of a white child having been taken away at the same time. She could, when brought in, speak nothing but Lushai.

Orders received from Government directed the two columns to effect a meeting, if possible, before retiring from the country, but added that there might be more important objects for them to carry out, and under any circumstances the columns were to be back at Cachar and Chitta-gong respectively by the 10th March.

From telegrams received from General Brown-low, conveying information of his whereabouts and intended movements, it seemed highly improbable that a junction of the two columns would be effected, and as the reduction of Laboora's people to submission was the most important object for the Left Column to carry out, and the time was running short, the General decided to remain at Chelam till twelve days' supplies were raised there, and then, with the force " flying light " as possible, to make a hurried descent on Lalboora, reduce him to submission, and return at once.

Notice of this intended plan of operations was telegraphed to Brownlow, with the approximate latitude and longitude of Chumfai, and the probable date of arrival there; and also the intimation that on two consecutive nights rockets and blue lights would be fired from our camp, in the hope that, if General Brownlow could see them, communication by signalling might be effected.

On the 11th January, Colonel Rattray, with a wing of the 42nd, arrived at Chelam, to occupy the camp, which had been slightly stockaded; and from the 42nd the strength of the 44th and 22nd was made up to four hundred, who, with the Artillery, formed the force the General intended to take on with him.

In order to relieve the Commissariat as far as possible, and to facilitate the return march, all ponies and all servants, except one for each officer, were sent back to Chepui. All the coolies were employed during the halt in bringing up supplies from the rear.

Rice in large quantities, yams, beans, and many domestic articles were found hidden away about a mile from camp, in a large cave on the hill-side, through which a tiny stream of water trickled; and close to this stream was a small basket, containing a little rice suspended from a small two foot bamboo. On one side of the basket hung a slight diamond-shaped framework on which were twisted cotton threads, red, black, and white, the representation of a stockade about a foot high, behind which were arranged little lumps of clay pinched up into the semblance of men without legs, completing the arrangement by which I suppose the Lushais thought to propitiate their gods, and secure their protection for this concealed property.

In this cave was a very fine collection of antlers. Foraging parties also discovered large quantities of rice in many places around; this was all brought into camp and husked, the Lushais being paid for it at a fair rate.

While still at Chelam we heard that the Munipur contingent had been obliged to retire from Chibu, in consequence of the ever increasing difficulty of getting up supplies, and having lost more than half their number from sickness and desertion.

This, it was feared, might give General Bourchier more trouble in his advance on Chumfai, as the Lushais, released from watching the contingent, would be able to concentrate their forces to oppose our column ; but it was not known what their action would be after we left Chelam.

Rumours reached us of a strongly fortified place not very far from Chelam, where, if we were opposed at all, it was probable that the Lushais would make a stand.

On the 11th Darpong came in with several of his countrymen, and informed us that Lalboora, leaving the village to its fate, had taken refuge among the Pois, and that no further opposition was intended.

Lalboora's mother, we were also informed, had

done all she could from the first to induce her
sons to submit, and they had consented to grant
all our demands. This was all very satisfsctory,
but no one knew how far it was reliable, and on
the 12th the force, composed of the troops before
detailed, marched from Chelam camp.

The weight of the Sepoys' baggage was now
reduced to one half, the officers' baggage to a
couple of blankets as bedding, one change of
raiment, and a few cooking utensils. Everyone
was pleased to be once more on the move after the
nine days' halt, and all were looking forward
to a speedy conclusion of the campaign.

Before starting, Mr. Edgar heard that Poiboi
had actually come into the village to meet us;
but that, having got so far, his courage again
failed, and the desired interview did not take place.

The road beyond Chelam bore the appearance
of being much used, and in the steeper parts
steps were cut. One curious fact about the
Lushai paths is that, if a tree falls across one, they
never take the trouble to remove it, but merely
cutting foot-holds in it, allow it to remain where
it fell.

S

About a mile from camp we came to a leafy ravine, with a little stream running through it. It was spanned by a picturesque bridge, formed by the large truuk of a single tree, supported by small trestles with a bamboo roadway, creepers brought down from the trees above serving as additional ties and supports for the handrails.

. Not far beyond this we passed the remains of a very large Lushai encampment, and a little further on heard two shots fired in front, and thought we were in for a little excitement. These, however, turned out only to be signal shots from scouts on the watch in the villages ahead, giving intimation that the troops were on the road.

About noon we passed through a village containing about thirty-eight houses, called Raimang, prettily situated on the slopes of the hill, crowning a very steep precipice. The villagers had gone into the jungle on our approach, but, on signs being made to some who were visible, they returned.

The march thence was continued along the hillside through extensive jooms, finally descending towards afternoon to the level grassy valley of the Dimlui, a clear, pretty little stream.

Here we were joined by some villagers from Tulcheng, a village a little ahead, which we had seen from Chelam. At this village the General determined to encamp for the night, and after a short halt the force again addressed itself to the hill.

About four P.M. we found ourselves in a deep ravine which had been prepared for a most formidable defence. A very strong stockade occupied an excellent position, commanding the road for two or three hundred yards from the opposite side of the ravine, the passage of which had been rendered almost impossible by a number of large felled trees, so entangled together as completely to impede our route.

The hill to the right ran up to about four or five hundred feet above the road, and on this slope several small stockades and breast-works afforded flank defence to the principal one, and would have rendered very difficult any attempt to turn it; while it could not have been taken with a rush, as the troops floundering through the dense and

s 2

tangled mass would have been exposed to fire from the stockade in front, and at the same time to the heavy fire sweeping the ravine from these flankers. Moreover, there was no very suitable position from whence the artillery could have opened fire.

These fortifications had, it was evident, been only recently prepared for the express purpose of opposing our advance, and indeed had not been quite completed when Lalboora made up his mind not to fight. The path had been cleared again when we arrived; and the troops pulled down the principal stockade. Then passing on through a narrow defile, we came upon a second smaller and less strong stockade. The path wound between small eminences, several crowned with timber breastworks, so that if the Lushais had chosen to defend this ravine, we should have had all our work cut out for us; and considering the lateness of the hour at which we arrived, we could hardly have made ourselves masters of the situation before dark.

This was the most strongly fortified position we had met with in the country. It was evident, I think, that the Lushais, remarking the comparative ease with which we turned a single stockade across the road, treating it with the greatest contempt, saw the necessity of some further flank defences; and certainly the man who chose this position and planned these fortifications might, under more favourable circumstances and among a more civilized people, have become a Todtleben or a Burgoyne.

CHAPTER XVII.

THE TRUE POIBOI—DEFENCES OF THE VILLAGE OF TULCHENG—
SCARCITY OF WATER—ROMANTIC STORY OF TWO CHILDREN—
VALLEY OF OF THE LUI-TAO—HEAVY FIRING HEARD—LETTER-
WRITING UNDER DIFFICULTIES—INGENIOUSLY CONSTRUCTED
GATE.

CHAPTER XVII.

THE villagers had requested the General, as all their women and children were there, not to occupy the village. Since the fire at Chelam, he had determined not to halt in a village, and so he readily acceded to their request, only requiring them to bring out some material for huts, which they did.

As it was about six o'clock by this time, the troops were not able to hut themselves. Waterproof sheets and tarpaulins were hastily rigged up. We had a large tarpaulin for our instruments, and this with a waterproof sheet formed a very fair shelter, underneath which we squeezed in between theodolite, plane-table, &c., the inequalities and slope of the ground being rectified in some degree by bags of rice, atta, &c., (our coolies' rations) which, however, made a lumpy place of rest.

The day's march had been a trying one. Though only nine miles in actual distance, it had occupied nine hours in time, owing to the steep ascents and descents, and the narrowness of the path, along which the force slowly wound its way in single file, with frequent checks and halts. We saw a very handsome sago-palm during the journey, the first we had seen in these hills.

The next morning we started again at nine o'clock. The villagers at first objected to our passing through the village itself, but a compromise was effected by sending the coolies round.

Darpong told Mr. Edgar early in the morning that Poiboi, who had followed us from Chelam and halted during the night at the Dimlui, was then in the village. Mr. Edgar sent Hurri Thakoor, (his right-hand man and interpreter, familiarly known as Harry Tucker), with Engloom and another Lushai fugitive, to identify him.

He turned out to be the true Poiboi this time. He promised to be faithful to us for the future, but was very nervous during the interview, and, like some timid animal, darted off now and then towards the jungle, as if he feared being caught by some stratagem, notwithstanding the assurances of his muntri that there was no danger of this.

Afterwards, as Mr. Edgar was watching the coolies passing the village from the height above, Darpong told him that Poiboi was on an adjoining hill and wanted to see him. Mr. Edgar replied that the chief must go to see the General, who had ridden on; but this he could not be prevailed on to do, and thus the last chance of an interview with the chief was lost.

Poiboi was a very young man, about twenty years of age, and had been so much impressed by the history of Lalchokla, that he could not bring himself to believe in our promises to respect his liberty, especially after implicating himself in the affair of the 25th.

The village of Tulcheng was surrounded by a very strong stockade, which was defended against escalade by a thick hedge of brushwood running all along the top, in which were firmly secured bamboo stakes inclining outwards and downwards. The entrances were defended by strong gates, which were made of thick planks, each cut out of one tree, with a large projecting piece left at the back, through which the securing bar was passed. Each plank was pivoted at the top and bottom in a strong framework of timber.

A short distance from the village the path went over a steep bit of rock, about twelve feet high, the descent being accomplished by a rickety bamboo ladder which delayed the troops considerably. The Goorkhas, in their thick boots, were very nervous in crossing such places, whereas without their boots they ran up and down them like cats. The coolies fortunately found another and easier route from the village.

We discovered another very handsome specimen of the sago palm in the ravine beyond this rocky descent.

Crossing the ravine, the road ascended and ran along the edge of a very steep precipice, and continued along the range without any very great descent. There was great difficulty in finding water, mile after mile being traversed without meeting even a trickle. At last, towards evening, we came out on a large grassy level, with an elevation of about six thousand feet, overlooking the entrance to Lalboora's country.

The scene was a very fine one. Heavy clouds hung over the pass, on each side of which Dilk-lang aud Murklang rose to a height of nearly seven thonsand feet, dark and frowning, while between and beyond lay the valley of the Tui-tao; and far away the high mountains of the Soktés and Burmese rose against the sky, softly lighted up by a few level rays of the declining sun, which struggled through a distant break in the dark clouds.

Soon after we found water, a very scanty supply, and far from our camping ground, near a small deserted village, called Buljung, situated on a spur of the Dilklang, formally inhabited by Lenkom's people. Here we encamped after another nine miles of tedious march.

The small supply of water was our great grief, but we hoped to get down to the river, in the valley, the next day, and so made the best of it. A pint of water was the allowance for four for washing in next morning, a solemn compact being made that no soap was to be used till each had dipped his face.

A military authority, I forget who, writing on campaigning, says, " Officers will be astonished to find what a very small amount of washing is necessary to their happiness," or words to that effect, and we had often occasion to acknowledge the truth of the remark. " The means to do ill deeds make ill deeds done," and though washing hands is not exactly an ill deed, yet the fact of having soap and water at hand, I have no doubt, is often the cause of an unnecessary washing of these members.

The evening of our arrival at Buljung, we were joined by two little children, a boy and girl, of the Sadoé tribe, with a very romantic history. They had lived with their father and three other children in a village about ten miles off. The Sadoés, in this village, had been detained there against their will by the Lushais, and they took advantage of the presence of the Contingent, at Chibu, to effect their escape.

On the night of the villagers' exodus, the father took his three young children on his back and in his arms, the two elder ones following. In the darkness and confusion, the poor little things missed their father and lost themselves in the jungle, in which they wandered for several days, living on roots and berries.

At length they reached a village, where they heard of the approach of our column, and that their maternal uncle was with it. When they heard that the force was at Tulcheng, they started for Buljung, and awaited our arrival there. They remained with us, and accompanied us on the return to Cachar.

The next day, February 14th, a slight shower fell about six a.m., but soon cleared off again, and we marched at the usual hour, descending the west face of Dilklang, to the east of which rises the Tui-tao, probably a tributary of the Koladyne, if not the Koladyne itself. We descended some seventeen hundred feet into the flat alluvial valley of the Tui-tao, which joins the Teo about six or seven miles south of Buljung. The valley is very level, as its name implies, Tui " water," Tao " sitting." We found that we had crossed the water parting at Dillang, and that thenceforth the streams flowed in a southerly direction.

Our path lay along the banks of the river for about three miles, crossing it repeatedly, and passing through tall reeds and wormwood. Our march was a short one, about five miles altogether, and very easy.

We arrived at our halting place, where a small stream joined the Tao, about one p.m., and forthwith set about to build little huts. Plenty of trees, with large leaves, and grass growing in this spot, we had no difficulty in speedily constructing our shelter; and then proceeded in a body to enjoy the luxury of a bathe in a wide pool, among large stones, where the river widened slightly. We took down a change of raiment, and having bathed ourselves, we proceeded to wash our discarded suits, each officer becoming his own dhobi with much satisfaction to himself—having so much water to play with being really a treat.

This camp became "No. 17 Station," and a halt was made on the 15th to give the coolies a rest, which they much needed, as many had only returned to Chelam with supplies the day before we started, and the two long marches to Tulcheng and Buljung and want of water had knocked them up.

In the morning some Lushais scouts, who had been sent on the day before to reconnoitre, returned with the tidings that heavy firing had been heard in the direction of Chumfai. They supposed it was caused by an attack on the village of Chonchim, in which Vonolel's widow lived, by some Soktés under Kamhow of Molbhem.

Some other Lushai were at once sent off to find out the real facts. During the day a great many of Lenkom's people, and some Pois subject to that chief, came in bringing presents.

It was fortunate that we did halt here this day, as heavy clouds had been gathering all the morning, and about eleven A.M. a regular downfall commenced, which lasted till five P.M., detaining us inside our huts, endeavouring to keep ourselves and property dry—a difficult matter, as the rain found out some weak place in the roof or waterproof sheets every five minutes. We solaced

T

ourselves with cold pork and pickles, and wrote home letters under difficulties.

The next day was a very fine one—indeed the Expedition was very fortunate as regards the weather throughout; not getting rain more than four of five times, and then only on the halt. The first night at Daidoo was the only occasion on which we were seriously inconvenienced by it.

Immediately on leaving camp we began to ascend the Murklang, and after a steep climb of three thousand feet, reached a small village of Paites or Soktés, who had been settled there by Vonolel. This village was situated close to the edge of a very precipitous cliff, and was strongly stockaded; the approaches from the south being also stockaded.

The construction of the gate to the principal stockade was ingenious, though I am told it is common in all the hill districts of the Eastern frontier. It consisted of several thick uprights, which swung freely from a horizontal bar passing through their upper ends. These could be easily pushed aside to admit of anyone passing in or out, at the same time they were quickly secured on the inside by fixing a horizontal bar across them, about a foot from the ground.

We were met by the whole population, men, women, and children; among them were some very old men, including their head-man Engow. One white-haired old man, who said he was a hundred years old, and looked it, fell at the General's feet, and then rising, blessed him. They complained of the oppression of the Lushais, and said that ten armed men had been sent from their village to aid the Lushais in the attack of the 25th. They had been induced to do this, as they had heard fearful tales of the cruelties to which we should subject them if we got as far as their village; but when they heard how different was our real treatment of those by whom we were unopposed, they refused to join in defending the stockade at Tulcheng when called upon by Lalboora and the other chiefs, saying, " Why, for your sakes, should we oppose people who will harm neither us nor our property if we do not oppose them ?"

This was also the answer given by the inhabitants of several other subject villages, and it is probable that this defection influenced in some measure Lalboora's decision not to fight.

We learned also from these villagers that the Soktés had attacked Chonchim, but had been beaten off with the loss of four of their number; one Lushai had been killed, and four wounded.

From the village the pathway ran along the east face of Murklang, a rocky precipice, clothed here and there with trees and grass, having a sheer descent of some thousand feet. Beneath nestled a small village, and beyond lay the broad and smiling valley, through which far below, like a silver thread, the Teo wound its way. High hills of dark green, on the slopes of which the jooms shone like gold in the bright sunshine, rose in the background.

The beauty of the scene was heightened by the rhododendrons which clothed the hill-side on either side of the road, and were then in all their glory of brilliant blossoms, and helmets and turbans became gaily decorated. Even the guns were not forgotten; their prosaic steel forms being also adorned with the bright flowers, with almost loving care, by their Sikh gunners.

Shortly after we passed through a magnificent pine forest; a gentle breeze sighing through the tall pines wafted their sweet perfume across our onward path. We passed two deserted villages without meeting with any water, and finally descended into the Chumfai valley, where we encamped very late in the evening, having covered nearly thirteen miles in the day's march. Messengers were at once sent on to Chonchim, requiring the people to submit.

The valley of Chumfai is about five miles long, with an average breadth of a mile, and an elevation of four thousand nine hundred feet; the hills all round rising to a height of above one thousand or twelve hundred feet. The ground is swampy in many places, and low hills, covered with small leafless trees, are dotted over its surface.

This valley seems to have once been a lake, which has gradually silted up in the manner described by Captain Pemberton, with reference to the Loytak Lake in 1835.

" The bed has begun very perceptibly to fill up from deposits of silt, from the surrounding heights, which are continually carried into it, and if this process continues, a few years will suffice to obliterate the lake altogether."

" There runs in the lake a range of low hills, the portions of which, not covered with water, form islands.

The low hills in the Chumfai valley, which now look isolated, are probably peaks of a similar low range which ran through the lake, the alluvial deposit having taken the place of the water in covering up the lower portions of this range. The soil of this plain seems to be fertile, but is at present uncultivated.

CHAPTER XVIII.

VONOLEL'S VILLAGE—VONOLEL'S TOMB—PLEASING TRAIT IN A
DOCTOR—BUILDING OPERATIONS—CONDITIONS OF PEACE—
FRATERNISING—MADAME RACHEL'S WIDELY-SPREAD REPU-
TATION—OUR INTERCOURSE WITH THE LUSHAIS—LIGHTING
PIPES—EXPERIMENTS WITH THE BURNING GLASS.

CHAPTER XVIII.

THE next day, February 17th, the force marched about four miles to the other end of the valley, where on some long broad spurs of a high hill stood Lungvel, the village of Vonolel. This village we found deserted,. and it had the appearance of having been so for some time, the houses being in a tumble-down state. It had been a very large village, and was said to have contained a thousand houses, but only about half that number were remaining when we arrived.

We found Vonolel's tomb on an open elevated spot—a similar erection to Voupilal's tomb, already described. This, however, was more elaborate and in a better state of preservation, and the posts around, kept in their places by a horizontal bar, supported a perfect forest of horns and heads. Inside the tomb a broken Burmese idol was placed in state, and in the centre was a post bearing a very large metua skull, from one of the horns of which a human head and arm, recently cut off, were suspended, and beneath, just outside the tomb, we found a foot.

The unfortunate whose head and limbs these were, we afterwards learned was one of the Soktés killed in the attack on Chonchim two days before. The eyes had been torn out, the skull smashed, and shot-marks and spear-cuts disfigured the face, which in life must have been a very pleasing one. A doctor with us went up to inspect the head, and exclaimed with the greatest indignation :

" What confounded brutes !"

" Humane man, pleasing trait in a doctor," was the thought that suggested itself to his hearers, till he further enlightened them as to the cause of his humane anger.

" They have actually smashed the skull, and I would have given anything for it for my museum."

In fact all the medicos with us were quite as eager for Lushai skulls as any Lushai could have been for theirs ; though, in the interests of civilization, the Lushais' heads would have reposed in glass cases on velvet cushions probably, while those of our friends would have been elevated on poles exposed to the wind and the rain.

When all the troops had come up, they were formed up in a hollow square in front of the tomb, and the British flag was hoisted on a tall, bare tree—" on a spot where British flag had never before fluttered in the breeze."

The General addressed his little force in a few well-chosen and appropriate sentences ; telling them that at last the goal had been reached, and we stood in Vonolel's stronghold. Then thanking them in behalf of the Queen and Viceroy for their admirable behaviour throughout, he concluded by saying that little more remained to be done before the force would commence the homeward march.

At the close of this address three hearty cheers were given in the true British fashion ; then the Sepoys invoked their gods in their peculiar manner ; and the shouts of triumph must have struck terror into the hearts of the Lushais who crowded the village of Vonolel's widow on a high neighbouring hill, whence from afar they could watch the invader, and must have impressed those who still counselled opposition with the futility of resisting this confident foe.

While the troops were drawn up before the tomb they were photographed by Captain Cookesley, who was afterwards engaged in taking a photograph of the tomb when the village was fired. The Sepoys told off for this duty lighted the lower houses to windward first, contrary to orders, and poor Cookesley suddenly found himself surrounded by the flames, and had a narrow escape from losing all his apparatus.

The tomb was not destroyed, but the head and arm of the Sokté were removed and buried, and I trust he is happier in consequence.

The troops were withdrawn to the valley below, and encamped there along the banks of the little stream flowing through it, which rises in the hills near the village. This camp was in a very pleasant spot, dry, open, and grassy, under large bare trees; the ground beneath being covered with their withered leaves. The whole scene reminded one strongly of some woodland landscape at home in winter time, especially in the early morning, when the hoar-frost still lies white upon leaf and grassy blade.

The village and the grassy mounds supplied us with plenty of materials for hutting ourselves very comfortably. A great many excellent planks were found in the houses; and one officer, on the principle of doing as the Lushais do, erected a stockade of planks round his little sleeping-place, and decorated the entrance with a huge metua head, a little monkey's skull also grinning between the horns.

While these building operations were going on, the head-men of Chonchim came into camp, but were refused an audience till they could give up some of the plunder taken from Monirkhal, &c.

During the evening, a policeman's musket, pouch, and coat, the coat of a Sepoy of the 4th N.I. killed at Monirkhal, and some brass vessels were brought in and delivered up, with a promise that other articles should follow.

The head-men were then told that the General intended to visit their village next day, and they would be required to attend in camp beforehand to hear the terms imposed upon them, and to accompany the General to the village.

Scattered about near our camp, we found several curious stones about six feet long. Each of the latter was generally rudely carved with a figure of a man holding a daô and spear, with a gourd and metua head near. On one stone about fifteen little figures were cut, holding hands, as if "going round the mulberry bush," or some similar dance.

I could not find out if these were graves; I believe they were not, but only a kind of com- memorative stones.

The next morning, the 18th February, the head-men appeared in camp, and the terms decided on by the General and Mr. Edgar in consultation, were stated to them.

Firstly—If they were unable to produce Lal- boora (who was said to have taken refuge among the Pois), three head-men of the village should accompany the column as hostages as far as Tipai Mukh.

Secondly—That they should agree to receive

agents of Government in their villages when demanded.

Thirdly—That they should restore all firearms taken at Monirkhal and the Nudigram ; and if they were unable to collect the full number of twelve at once, that they should give up that number of their own weapons, which could afterwards be re-exchanged.

Fourthly—That they should deliver as a fine, a war-drum, a set of gongs, large and small, an amber necklace, two large tusks, four metuas, ten goats, ten pigs, fifty fowls, and twenty maunds of husked rice.

The head-men were also informed that in case these two last conditions were not complied with before the morning of the 20th, their village would be attacked and destroyed. They at first declared they were too hard, and Darpong, flying into a passion, said he wished to go home.

The General replied that the head-men might take their choice between submission and the destruction of their village; and told Darpong he was quite at liberty to go home if he wished. This brought him to his senses, and he did not go

Soon after this, the General, taking with him one hundred and fifty men, ascended the hill towards Chonchim. On the way we met some more of the head-men, who turned back with us. As we approached the village, we could see a large number of armed Lushais standing outside a stockade, on the open crest of the hill above. They shouted at us, and made various hostile demonstrations.

The Goorkhas were at once extended in skirmishing order, and advanced steadily, with sloped arms, up the steep ascent, which was very thinly wooded. At the same time, the head-men, evidently fearing a collision, ran on in front of us, calling out as they unwound turbans and sheets, and waved them wildly over their heads as they fled on up the hillside. Their words, and, probably, the determined manner in which the Sepoys advanced, not heeding in the slightest the Lushai muskets pointed at them, had the desired effect; and, as we advanced, the Lushais retired within the stockade.

Passing through this, a short walk brought us to the village, also strongly stockaded. Both

stockades bore the marks of the fight of a few
days before; the outer one being broken through
in one or two places, where the Soktés had
forced an entrance, and the stockade round the
village itself was pierced with many bullet-holes
near the gateway.

On the path we saw a large blood-stain, and
in the ravine below lay the corpse of a Sokté.
Arrived at the gate, we found all the Lushais
had withdrawn inside and shut it, and were
ranged along the stockade as if to defend it.

A parley ensued between the head-men and
the General, who drew up the troops facing the
stockade. The danger of another scrimmage
did not, even then, seem quite past; but, at
length, the General and officers with him, and
twenty Sepoys were admitted.

The muskets had been concealed as if by
magic, and all the houses were shut up. The
women and children had been removed to the
jungles, and below the village, guarding the
approach to their place of concealment, we could
see two armed Lushais pacing to and fro with
all the regularity and steadiness of a British

sentry; shewing in their grave and anxious faces their sense of a great responsibility.

We remained in the village about three hours, while Captain Badgley surveyed from a very favourable open spot, at the highest part of the village, the surrounding country; a confused sea of hills on all sides, among which it was exceedingly difficult, from this point of view, to recognise our old friends of the more northerly part of the country.

We could see far away to the west the high hills of the Howlong and Syloo tribes, where General Brownlow was doing battle with his refractory chiefs; and we hoped that he might be able to see our signals.

While Badgley was surveying, and the General and Mr. Edgar were explaining their terms, and the necessity for compliance with them, to the headman and the serious-minded portion of the community, the younger ones, with a happy carelessness of all negotiations, were making great friends among the invaders, with whom they had been within an ace of exchanging shots scarcely an hour before.

These men were much astonished at the fairness of our skins. The "world-wide fame of
Madame Rachel" seems to have penetrated even
to this remote corner of the globe; perhaps even
some of "the swift-pacing camels" have visited
Chumfai (and we have the authority of the
Graphic for believing that camels can climb the
Lushai hills, "all opinions of Indians to the
contrary notwithstanding)" for the purpose of
collecting the rare flowers and simples (over and
above those found at home), so necessary to
the art of "beautifying for ever." I say the
lady's fame seems to have reached even the
Lushais, as they evidently thought it was to some
such art as hers that we owed the comparative
fairness of our faces and hands. They made signs
to us to turn up our sleeves, when loud were their
cries of amazed delight at finding that the skin
above our wrists was actually whiter than our
hands. Even then some of the most sceptical
were not satisfied that the white would not come
off, till they had rubbed it well with wet fingers,
examining the latter after the process very carefully.

The Lushais were much pleased with the simple process of lighting a pipe or fuel by means of a burning glass ; and after a short time, to show them one was the signal for the instant production of pipes which had gone out. They themselves generally carry a rough flint and steel, and small pieces of rag in a small bamboo box.

They could not understand how the fire was brought down, and often put out their hands to feel the burning power of the glass when focussed upon them. After submitting to the experiment for a few seconds, they invariably drew back suddenly, with an exclamation of pain and surprise, intensely gratifying to their friends who had already tested the power of the burning-glass.

I have mentioned that the Lushais are not a tall or bearded race, and one of the officers, who was gigantic in stature, with a long thick beard, was looked upon by them as a most wonderful being. It was intensely amusing to see them stealing up behind him one by one, when they thought his attention was engaged with something in front, and, stretching up one hand and arm at full length, stand on tip-toe while they tried to reach

the level of the top of his helmet. Sometimes by a
sudden and judicious application of his elbow he
sent them sprawling, much to the amusement of
those who had accomplished their object without
detection. Others measured the length of his
beard on their arms.

When pointing out a hill or other distant object,
the Lushais give vent to a curious long note,
gradually dying away, to express something very
far off, before mentioning the name of the hill, &c.,
very much as I have heard Scotch friends of
mine on similar occasions say—

"That hill far awa-a-a-ay."

In the open space above referred to, we saw the
stump of a large tree used as a beheading-block.
there were traces on it of a recent execution,
brains and hair, and the villagers explained by
signs that the Sokté, whose head they pointed
to on the distant tomb, had been executed there,
and showed us a small stick with which his
eyes had been prised out.

They appeared to view the whole as a most
praiseworthy performance, and indeed the treatment of traitors and prisoners in our own country,

in ages when the English were regarded as being
much more enlightened than the Lushais are
now, was often very little, if at all, better than
theirs.

CHAPTER XIX.

DELIVERY OF THE FINE—DIFFICULTY IN COLLECTING THE
MUSKETS—ACCEPTABLE CHANGE OF DIET—THE COMMISSA-
RIAT—AUSTRALIAN MUTTON—A COOLIE TRICK—LUSHAI
RAIDS—THE TRAGEDY AT PORT BLAIR—RETURN MARCH.

CHAPTER XIX.

ABOUT four o'clock the force fell in to return to camp—Mr. Edgar repeating his terms once more outside the gate on leaving, and stating that the muskets must be given up and the fines paid within twenty-four hours. Three of the head-men returned with us.

It was a beautiful afternoon, the soft breeze playing among the oaks and rhododendrons, as we waded on our way down the hill to the pretty little valley beneath. When we neared the camp the sun was setting, and the tall trees and low hillocks cast long purple shadows over the golden surface of the plain.

The next day several parties were sent out in various directions to search for villages. Several were seen, but all at great distances.

From the heights to the east of Chumfai, we could see the open smiling valley of the Teo, and if time had permitted, it would have been worth while following its course in order to settle the question as to its really being the Koladyne itself, or simply an affluent of that river.

During the day portions of the fine were brought in, but the General refused to receive anything till the muskets were all delivered. The Lushais promised they should all be produced during the night.

The Lushais in the village, who possessed weapons of their own, were naturally averse from losing them, and cast lots as to whose should be given up. This did not always meet the case though, for as soon as the lot fell upon a man, he straightway disappeared into the jungle, taking his musket with him. All this, as the head-man complained, prevented the tale of muskets from being speedily completed. However, during the night they were all collected, and with the fine imposed upon them, were received into camp. The three muntris who were to accompany us as hostages, were also chosen at the same time.

Although all the terms which could be immediately enforced had been complied with by the villagers, and nothing more remained for the force to accomplish, yet it was decided to halt one day longer in Chumfai, partly to impress the Lushais with the idea that we were in no hurry to depart, and could have remained longer if we had chosen; but principally because our work had been done in less time than was anticipated when we left Chelam, and by marching on the 20th, we should not have been able to signal to General Bourchier on that night from Chumfai, as he had been informed, by telegram, we should do. So it was decided to remain till the morning of the 21st, sending up rockets from one of the highest peaks east of Lungvel, and marching, on the 21st, to the summit of Murklang to send further signals from that hill.

Portions of the fine, such as the fowls, pigs, &c., were distributed among the officers and men, and were very acceptable as a change after the tinned mutton and salt pork, which, also, at this period, were running rather short, as, indeed, had been the case once or twice before;

and if we had not occasionally been able to get a few small tins of stores down by the dâk, we should, more than once, have had nothing but rice during the day. Pickles were generally procurable; but regarded as the staple of diet for several days, they pall upon the least fastidious taste.

I must do the Commissariat Officers the justice to say that, amid all their troubles and anxieties, they invariably received complainants with the greatest politeness. The *suaviter in modo* was never wanting in their godowns, though the mutton in tins occasionally was.

We were much amused at reading, in a home paper about this time, a letter from the Secretary of some Soup Society, complaining that an old pauper woman had refused to eat some Australian mutton he had given her, as being unfit for human food, and had returned it without thanks. We occasionally wished, when in a more than usually British grumbling mood, that this estimable old lady could have been placed on the Committee in Calcutta, when the question of rations was being considered, before starting the Expedition. Perhaps, though, as the Committee merely had to decide what others should eat and drink, she might not have expressed her opinion so forcibly.

The coolies once, bringing up some rum to the front, drank half of it, and filled up the casks with water. This was brought to the notice of the Commissariat Officer thus. He had just come in from a long march, and was sitting down in camp, waiting for the coolies and servants, when an officer offered him some rum and water, which he accepted. He tasted it, said it was " very weak," and asked to see the rum bottle. He put it to his lips, and without winking drank the contents, the owner's allowance for several days, nearly all off. Then handing it back to the officer, he said, with a suave little motion of the head :

" Ah, dear me! dear me! oh yes! I see, you carry your rum and water ready mixed, Well! well! a very good plan."

However, he was astonished to hear that this bottle had only just been filled from a Commissariat cask, and inquiry resulted in the discovery of the coolies' malpractices.

The fact of the plunder taken at Monirkhal being found in Lalboora's villages was very satisfactory; for though Mr. Edgar had long been certain of it, still others, and some high in authority, had doubted if the Left Column was taking the right direction for finding the principal offenders.

Mr. Edgar learnt from the head-men that all the Lushais considered that " this village of Vonolel's gave the signal for every raid; even for those conducted by independent chiefs; and that the plunder taken in the last raids had all been taken first to Chumfai, and then distributed among the other villages." In the afternoon the gunners were sent up the hill fixed upon as the best from which to fire off the signals, and made their arrangements for the evening.

The Lushais in camp were allowed to accompany them to witness the spectacle; and when at last, about eight o'clock, the blue lights burned and the rockets went up, these unwashed Lushais expressed their admiration with exactly the same cries of " Oh! Oh!" by which our own great unwashed at home are in the habit of evincing the satisfaction with which they behold a beautiful display at the Crystal Palace. No response was elicited from the dim and misty hills where General Bourchier was supposed to be, and the Artillery returned after waiting a sufficient time for the other column to reply.

During the evening came the first rumours of the terrible tragedy at Port Blair, which we could scarcely believe, but which were afterwards too fully confirmed.

Many of the staff-officers had the honour of being personal friends of the late Viceroy, but even those who had not, knew that in him they had lost one who took the greatest and most kindly interest in the welfare of all engaged in the Expedition, an interest evinced in a most flattering telegram which the General had received on the subject of the successes of the 25th and 26th, concluding thus,

" Telegraph direct how you are."

This was only one out of many little proofs that he was watching attentively the progress of the Expedition, and not unmindful of the fate of those who were trying to make it successful. The calamity which the whole country was then deploring, cast a gloom over the termination of the campaign, and considerably lessened the anticipated joyousness of the homeward march.

The next morning, amid much calling upon their gods, with many signs of rejoicing on the part of the Sepoys, and probably no less to the satisfaction of the Lushais, our troops commenced the return march.

Looking at them from the heights above, the line looked like a long serpent gradually uncoiling itself from the camp, soon extending nearly the whole length of the valley, and creeping slowly over hillocks and along the level plain ; a column of smoke from the fired camp proclaiming the departure of the rear-guard.

We camped that evening on Murklang, and further signals were sent up, also without any response. The villagers came out and mixed with the Sepoys with the greatest confidence, and brought out materials for huts. These could only be very hastily constructed, and most of us rigged up waterproof sheets and tarpaulins as little tents. A heavy shower of rain fell about nine P.M., but fortunately did not last long.

But little more remains to be chronicled; the return march was made over the road and through the villages already described. The villagers at Tulcheng came out in crowds to greet us as we passed, but at Chelam great anxiety was visible among the people. This was caused by the failure of Colonel Rattray to induce Poiboi to appear in camp, and, consequently, they feared that the General would carry out his threat of destroying their villages.

They came into camp on the day the troops halted there, and besought him to spare them, saying should he still adhere to his resolution they would bring in their women and little children also to fall at his feet and pray for mercy.

The General yielded to their prayers. He felt, as indeed did everyone, that after our camp had been allowed to remain close to their villages for so long without any annoyance, and the coolies and dâk guards had daily passed to and fro without any molestation from the Lushais, it would be an ungenerous, as well as an ungraceful, act to burn their houses on our departure, especially after Poiboi's promise to be faithful to us. His refusal to see the General in person, the latter attributed, and no doubt rightly, to the abject fear of an unreasoning boy.

The troops halted one day at Chelam to allow the wing of the 42nd, who had been holding the camp, to go ahead, taking with them the sick and weakly.

Everyone was happy in the idea of returning, and the long steep marches were as nothing to what they had been during the advance. Of the Sepoys and coolies, who were well, it might be said that,

> " Up the mountains sides they'd press,
> Nor with a sigh their toil confess."

This was not the case with those unfortunates upon whom the hard work, long continued, had told severely, and who not only with sighs but deep groans expressed their feeling of toil, as, relieved from all loads, they yet crawled on with the greatest difficulty, each day adding to their number and filling the doolies with men not able to walk.

CHAPTER XX.

WITHDRAWAL OF THE TROOPS—SECOND HALT—DISTRIBUTION
OF PRESENTS—DARPONG'S WATCH—CABULI FRUIT-SELLERS
—LUSHAI ENTERTAINMENT—APPEARANCE OF THE COUNTRY
—DAK ARRANGEMENTS—THE RESCUED CAPTIVES—COOLIE
ENTERTAINMENTS—RETURN TO TIPAI MUKH—PROFITABLE
COMMERCE.

CHAPTER XX.

THE withdrawal of the troops was conducted most methodically, each detachment in turn leaving a few men as guard, vacating its post two or three hours before the head-quarters arrived.

At Chepui the second halt was made, and a great distribution of presents took place to those men who had hitherto accompanied us. Red shawls and blankets, gay carriage rugs, white shirts, turbans of all sorts, and strangest present of all, but truly British-like in its inappropriateness, aluminium crystal-backed two guinea watches, and a glass decanter, were given away to the gratified recipients.

Darpong became the proud possessor of a watch, which he flourished about, applying it to the ears of his less fortunate friends for them to hear it tick, and showing them how the works moved. Alas! two days after he had lost the key, the watch had stopped, and no one envied him his prize in the least.

If it were necessary to give them something to amuse them, and at the same time point a moral, some of those musical toys, in which, by turning a handle gently, a small regiment of soldiers (usually three) is made to appear and disappear across a mimic parade-ground to the soft pleasing sound of a simple strain, would, no doubt, have delighted them. The Politicals might have explained to the intelligent savages that the soldiers were our troops; the parade-ground, Lushai Country; the motive power necessary to bring the Sepoys into that country the raiding they so often had indulged in; and that the inevitable consequence of their turning the handle would be the re-appearance of the soldiers at whose departure they were then rejoicing.

At Chepui we saw some enterprising Cabuli fruit-sellers who had been down as far as Kung-nung with their stock of raisins, pistachio nuts, almonds and native fruits. Purchases were eagerly made from them, and mysterious whispers conveyed the invitation :

" Come and dine, we have a plum-pudding to night."

Such invitations had hitherto been so rare, that it was impossible to refuse them.

The night we were at Chepui, about eight o'clock, as we were sitting over our camp fire discussing the events of the day and rum and water, we heard strains of music, accompanying a wild monotonous chant, approaching the camp. We rose to see what it meant, and saw nearly the whole male population of Chepui coming up in procession, preceded by a few men playing drums, gourd instruments, and reed-pipes. At their head marched a staff-officer with a lantern, who had gone to conduct the procession past the sentries.

The Lushais halted in an open space, and officers, Sepoys, and Lushais formed a ring, in which it was intimated dancing was to take place. After a short song, intended to be an account of our doings, but whether complimentary or not no one possessed sufficient knowledge of the language to determine, the dancing commenced. One man came forward, and loosing his sheet fastened it in a roll round his waist, and placing a small corn cob on the ground to indicate the lady of his affections, commenced a sort of *pas d'extase*. With bent knees, and body inclined forwards, he kept time to the slow music by swaying to and fro, turning now to the right, now to the left, opening and closing his fingers. Occasionally this motion was varied by a few excited bounds backwards and forwards, and twisting and twirling.

When the first dancer was tired a second took his place, but there was very little change in the character of the dance.

The entertainment was given by the flickering light of a few lanterns, fixed in their owners' waistbelts, or placed in the ground at their feet. After rum had been served out with great impartiality to all the performers, and the dancers had begun to get excited, kicking over the lanterns, and covering everyone with dust, the General said, " Hold, enough !" and the assembly broke up.

During the march to Chumfai, we had been
disappointed at meeting so few wild-flowers in
these jungles. Violets, with little or no scent,
had been frequently found, especially in Chumfai
valley; but these violets, some heliotrope, cox-
comb, and a few other common flowering weeds,
were the only varieties of Lushai Flora we
had discovered.

On the return, however, our disappointment
was turned to delight, and had we remained
longer in the country, we should, probably, have
been well pleased with the flowers. Even their
wild-fruit trees were in blossom, tall trees
covered with a large white flower like a gera-
nium, others a blaze of scarlet blossoms; the
crimson rhododendrons enlivened the gloom of
the forest; a beautiful little green passion-flower
hung in festoons from the trees, the convolvulus
adorned the tangled briers, and through the long
grass by the roadside sprang up golden fern and
lilac flowers.

The days were gloriously fine. Butterflies, of
the most brilliant and varied hues, chased each
other through the shadowy glades, and along the

sunlit path; while beautiful little red and yellow
birds flitted from tree to tree, flashing through
the sunlight like pure gold.

Unfortunately, owing to the rapid movements
of the troops, and to prevent any unnecessary
alarm or disturbances no one with the head-
quarters was allowed to shoot any birds in the
jungle. A native Naturalist had been sent from
Calcutta to accompany the Expedition, but he
remained in rear, and I do not know what addi-
tions he made to the Museum in the cause of
science.

We found that all the camps had been much
improved by those who had been stationed in
them. Commodious and well-built huts, small
mess-rooms, slight stockades, and well-cleared
spaces all round, made them hardly recognisable
as the little leafy shed-covered spots which we
used to come upon suddenly out of the jungle.

At one of the camps, a quantity of empty ghi
casks were thrown into the fires as the troops
were about to march. Having been well satu-
rated with their greasy contents, they blazed up
merrily, the iron hoops falling off into the flames

and exciting the cupidity of the Lushais, who, as usual, had collected to pick up anything the troops left behind them.

At first they tried to snatch out the hoops, but getting their clothes singed in the attempt, they retired to the jungle, and flinging everything off, armed themselves with long sticks, and rushed down upon the fires again; and as the rear-guard marched off, they saw the Lushais dancing and gesticulating like demons round the flames, red hot hoops being whisked out in all directions.

Our return was the signal for the commencement of jooming operations, the fires following us closely. Looking back each day, we could see their smoke rising up from the hill-sides, even to the camps we had left only that morning.

All the country for miles around was misty with joom smoke, and the increasing haze of the weather told of the approaching heat and rains. The view from each of our elevated camps was far less extensive than formerly, and many of the distant ranges had disappeared altogether.

On the journey back, at first, we used to get our

letters two and sometimes three times a day; not less than the number of deliveries in a well-conducted town in England. The reason of this was that each day we advanced a stage in the direction whence the letters were coming; so that we received letters before starting, and then reaching the following stage found the next dâk returning.

Here I must express my admiration for the dâk arrangements made by Colonel Roberts, and carried out under his orders by the police with wonderful regularity. Not a day passed without despatching the dâk, and scarcely a day without receiving the letters and papers, though they arrived sometimes in the middle of the night, much to the dissatisfaction of some drowsy souls, who preferred sleeping to any number of communications from friends.

A few souvenirs were brought away by the officers and men, such as skin shields, spears, musical instruments, &c., but the greatest curiosities of all which we brought back were the old captives who had been given up.

We had a large and increasing following of captives as we returned. Many of them were young people with their families, but among them were a few aged ladies and gentlemen, who were wonderfully old, and utterly incapable of walking. These were therefore carried on coolies' backs. The old things knelt in a sling which passed across the coolies' foreheads, and clung to his shoulders. This mode of travelling must have been very tiring in a long day's march.

When put down during a halt, they at once went to sleep, and seemed utterly apathetic as to their fate. A return to their native villages must have been for them the awaking of Rip Van Winkle; they would find young people become old, and all their former intimates dead or unmindful of them; and probably, if they had not been in the imbecility of extreme old age, would sooner have remained with their captors, who must have treated them with some consideration or kindness.

I made a sketch of one of these old people, but could arrive at no conclusion as to the age or sex, and my questioning elicited no response whatever from the shrivelled mummy. There was an expression of coarseness, and the reflection of far off sadness, as it were, visible in the countenance of the poor old thing, and one was filled with pity to think that it had still to be carried over a hundred miles, to find probably at the end no one to care for it or look after it, till welcome death should at last arrive.

Our coolies, who were Cossyahs, were very much pleased at the idea of returning home, and used occasionally in the evening to get up small entertainments of singing, whistling, and dancing round a fire. One, a little boy, used to arrange his dress like a woman's, and give imitations of Hindustani and Cossyah nautches to the accompaniment of an imaginary tom-tom. Their friends meanwhile looked on with an absence of any apparent approval, and a persistent gravity which could not have been surpassed by the most fashionable audiences at home, when viewing an amateur performance by their most enthusiastic friends.

Leeches, ticks, mosquitoes, sand-flies, and other abominations which we had been so freely promised by some sanguine friends before we started on the Expedition, but from which we had hitherto been free, began to annoy us very much on the return, and we were not sorry to get back once more to Tipai Mukh, where the whole force arrived on the 6th or 7th March.

The detachments from the nearer stations had gone on to Cachar on rafts or in boats as they arrived at Tipai Mukh, and the rest were employed in constructing rafts.

It had originally been intended that the troops should march, but owing to the heat, and the fact that cholera had once more appeared among the men at Tipai Mukh, the water-route seemed to be the best.

A large number of Lushais had accompanied us as far as Tipai Mukh, and were busily employed in driving a few last bargains. They brought down large quantites of India-rubber, which they exchanged eagerly for salt, equal weights, and as the value of the rubber was more than four times that of the salt, any individuals who could command a large supply of the latter had an excellent opportunity of doing a little profitable business.

By the 10th of March, in accordance with the orders of the Government before quoted, all the troops and coolies had bidden farewell to Tipai

Mukh ; and the Tuivai itself, flowing past ruined huts and deserted godowns, once more greeted the Barak with its ceaseless babble, undisturbed by the cries of coolies and the trumpeting of elephants, while the surrounding jungles relapsed into their former silence, resounding no more to the blows of the invaders' axes.

The rapids on the Barak, at this season of the year, were very shallow, and great excitement and amusement were afforded to the Sepoys by the trouble and hairbreadth escapes they met with in managing, or rather in trying to manage, their rafts, and steering them clear of sunken rocks and tree trunks.

This mode of travelling was entirely new to many of them, and their efforts were not always successful, as evinced by the ever-increasing pile of broken rafts at most of the difficult passages.

CHAPTER XXI.

——

HARDSHIPS OF THE CAMPAIGN—DEATH OF TWO OFFICERS—
INDISPOSITION OF THE GENERAL—RAVAGES OF CHOLERA
—THE MUNIPUR CONTINGENT—CONFERENCE—PRECAUTIONS
AGAINST TREACHERY — SEIZURE OF CHIEFS — FALSE PRE-
DICTION—ORDER TO THE TROOPS—CONCLUDING REMARKS.

Y

CHAPTER XXI.

I AM sorry to have to record two deaths
among the officers, in consequence of the
hardships of this campaign. One was Captain
Harrison of the 42nd N.I., who was about to proceed to England on sick leave when the Expedition
was determined on, and who immediately got his
leave cancelled in order to go with his regiment.
He was very ill at Tipai Mukh, at Christmas,
and the unhealthiness of the camp, which tried
many stronger constitutions, proved too much
for him, and he was ordered by the medical
authorities to proceed to England, viâ Calcutta,
as quickly as possible.

This was in February. He arrived in Cachar,
and was allowed by the doctor there to continue
his journey in the country boats. He was utterly

unfit to go alone, and when his boatmen went to inform him that they had arrived at Chuttack, they found him lying dead. His sad fate was deeply regretted by his brother officers, by whom he was deservedly very much liked.

The second was that of Captain Cookesley, R.A., whose name has been mentioned several times in the course of this narrative. A good photographer, he was attached to the half-battery which accompanied the column, partly in that capacity, being allowed extra carriage for his apparatus. He was apparently in tolerable health at Cachar, and went on with his battery as far as Sylhet, where he was obliged to go on shore, and was so ill as to be left there when the others continued the onward journey.

By the advice of the doctors he started to go to Shillong, the nearest hill-station to Sylhet. He arrived at Cherrapoonji, the first halting place from the plains, and, whether the change of temperature was too sudden, or nature at length gave way, I know not, but on the 31st March he expired at that place, shortly after his arrival, from abscess in the liver. A good officer, a genial companion, a clever writer, and a warm friend, his loss was mourned by all who had ever known him.

The General himself suffered severely at the close of the Expedition. The state of his health, between Tipai Mukh and Shillong, was such as to cause grave anxiety to the medical officers who accompanied him.

The bracing air of that fine hill station, a return to civilised dwellings, and, above all, good and nourishing food, however, happily soon restored him to his wonted health.

Several of the Staff, also, were very much pulled down, and did not get over the effects of hard work and hard fare for some time.

The scenery, both on the river and by road, between Tipai Mukh and Cachar, was very fine; the autumnal-like tints of the foliage in the dense jungle, at this season, were most varied and beautiful; orchids and other wild-flowers abounded, and the forest was sweet with their many-scented blossoms.

But an invisible foe haunted these fair scenes— and cholera, that fatal pestilence, stalked along the river, or lurked in the jungle, eager for his prey, striking down the Sepoys joyously looking forward to a speedy meeting with friends, but numbering most of its victims among the poor coolies, well nigh worn out with their four months continuous hard work. The poor fellows died alike on the river, in boats or on rafts; by the road-side and on the hill-tops, falling before a more dread enemy than any we had to encounter in Lushai land.

Nor were they free when they had left Cachar. The 22nd were pursued by it on their way up country, leaving men even in the train, and the 44th N.I. lost many men on the march before reaching Shillong.

The 42nd also suffered very severely. But among the sad consequences of the return march, was the introduction of this fell disease into tea-gardens and villages near the river or road, by the troops and coolies passing through. The seeds of the disease were left as a legacy among the Lushais, and, if we may believe reports, cholera has been busy among them since we left.

Hill-men dread the invasion of foreigners, more on this account perhaps than any other—I mean the introduction of strange diseases. Small-pox and other diseases have from time to time been spread among them by traders, though the Northern Lushais, with whom we had to do, had, hitherto, enjoyed apparent immunity from the consequences of intercourse with strangers, as, out of the many who visited our camps, we only saw one man at all marked with small-pox.

Before bringing this narrative to a close, we must just see what the Munipur Contingent had been doing, especially as their last exploit was a very peculiar one.

After the 25th of January, entire villages seeing the way things were going with the Lushais, and taking advantage of the presence of the contingent at Chepui, deserted to Munipur; others went to Kamhow, Sukpilal, and the Pois; but of those who went to Munipur, we have the actual numbers, which are as follows :

On the 13th February, three hundred and seventy-three Soktés, with twenty-eight muskets, arrived in Munipur, and on the 14th and 18th three hundred and ninety-two Sadoés and other Kookies.

I have mentioned that General Nuthall had been obliged to retire from Chibu, on account of sickness, &c. He had, however, returned there, towards the end of February, having received supplies, and left the sick in a place of safety. General Bourchier telegraphed to him on the withdrawal of the force from the Lushai territory, and General Nuthall commenced to return from Chibu on the 6th March.

On the 7th inst., he himself had gone ahead, as the Contingent always marched late, after cooking and eating. Before the latter left camp, a large body of men, of whom about a hundred were armed with muskets, appeared suddenly from the West.

Many captives, as before stated, having gone over to the Munipur contingent during the advance of the Left column, the Munipur Majors in command thought, or said they thought, that these were also refugees come to seek their protection. A Kookie chief who was in their camp, however, told them that the armed men belonged to Kamhow's people, and recognised among them a Chieftain of that tribe. The Majors sent orders to their Sepoys to load quietly and be on the alert; they then admitted the Soktés into the camp, taking up a central position, and a conference ensued.

During this conference the Sepoys closed round and got behind each armed man in groups of three. The Majors asked the Sokté chiefs where they had been, and whither they were going. They replied that they had been on a friendly visit to a village in the Lushai territory, the inhabitants of which, nine hundred and sixty-two in number, were returning with them, being desirous of joining Kamhow's tribe.

The Majors told them that they must go to General Nuthall to explain their conduct to him, but this they refused to do, as the camp ahead was too far out of their way. The former then apparently gave up this point and engaged the chiefs in friendly conversation, and under pretence of trying the different muskets, handed the chiefs one of theirs to fire off, discharging those of the latter in exchange.

The chiefs being thus defenceless, the Majors had them seized, whereupon, one of them giving a whistle, his men stood to their arms, but after a short struggle were overpowered. Fifty-six men were taken prisoners, and fifty-two muskets were seized; four of the Munipuris were wounded in the struggle.

The Sokté prisoners and the villagers were all taken into Munipur, and the Rajah intended to settle them in the valley south of Moirang. The Soktés were placed in jail in irons till their families should arrive, when the Rajah's intention was to release them and settle them in the hills north-east of the valley.

General Nuthall said, " The Rajah seemed confident of reconciling them, and anticipated obtaining much useful service from them in the event of future strife with Kamhow's tribe. The loss of so many arms to that tribe will tend to break its power, and restrain its preying upon the Lushais at this time of its weakness."

This latter prediction of the General's was a very mistaken one, if we may believe a late newspaper paragraph, which states that the Soktés again attacked Chonchim after our departure, and Lalboora, being deserted by many of his adherents, was signally defeated by the Soktés who are now settled in the Chumfai valley.

I have been unable to find out what truth there is in this report, but if the case is so, it is just what General Bouchier and Mr. Edgar did not wish to happen, and which by their policy they did what that they could to prevent; as it is, as I have pointed out in a very early part of this book, by no means in the interests of the peace of our frontier, that a tribe, who have submitted to us, and with whom we were likely to establish friendly relations, should be overthrown by a more distant and formidable foe.

We have heard the Munipur version of the exploit just related; let us see what has been said on the other side.

It will be remembered that Vonolel had settled many Sokté prisoners in his villages during his lifetime. These Soktés, at the time of the Expedition, were very anxious to return to their own country, but they were afraid that, if they attempted to escape, the Lushais might fall on them and kill their women and children before they could get safely across into Kamhow's country. Many of them had taken advantage of our advance to escape either to Kamhow, General Nuthall, or our camps.

On the return march, Mr. Edgar heard that a hundred armed men from Kamhow's villages had gone to some of the south-eastern Lushai villages, for the purpose of escorting the Soktés who wished to leave.

Darpong afterwards confirmed this intelligence, and stated further that nearly a thousand Soktés had gone off under the protection of this party, taking with them all their property, and that these were the people who appeared in the Munipur camp.

There seems no doubt that the armed Soktés did not go in with the intention of attacking the Munipur dépôt. This appears to be evident from the fact of their small number, and the absence of any attempt on their part at a surprise. On the contrary, they went in apparently in full reliance on the friendliness of the Munipuris, the chiefs allowing their weapons to be discharged by the Majors without any suspicion of bad faith.

Mr. Edgar, says, "The charge of wishing to attack the camp was probably afterwards invented by the Majors to excuse their own conduct. It is evident that the latter could not resist the temptation of getting possession of the refugees, for the Munipuris are even more eager than the hill-chiefs themselves to get hold of Kookie and Naga subjects."

Major McCulloch, many years ago writing of the Munipur Army, said that the number, three thousand six hundred (including officers), could not be kept up in an efficient state, and, as I have before said, it is not attempted. The services therefore of the Munipur troops in an emergency would be of no use. The inefficiency of this force has not escaped the British Government. Schemes for its improvement have been entertained, but as the pressure of circumstances which suggested the necessity of these schemes ceased, they have been discarded

I do not know if the performance of the Munipur contingent in the late campaign will cause the gallant Colonel to modify in any degree this unfavourable opinion.

On arriving in Cachar, General Bourchier issued the following Field Force Order to the troops who, having been together for four months, were about to separate and disperse again to various parts of India—the Artillery to Abbobabad, Sappers to Roorkee, 22nd N. I. to Chelam, and the 42nd and 44th L. I. to Assam.

(Gazette of India, May 4)

Field Force Order by Brigadier-General G. Bourchier, C.B., Commanding Cachar Column, Lushai Expeditionary Force— (No. 65, dated Cachar, the 19th March, 1872,)

1. On the breaking up of the Cachar Column, Lushai Expeditionary Force, the Brigadier-General Commanding feels deep pride in the reflection that he has received the congratulations of the late Viceroy, of the Governments of India and Bengal, and of His Excellency the Commander-in-Chief, on its services.

2. The Brigadier-General does not presume to offer an opinion as to whether the success of the column has equalled the expectations of the Government, but he has unfeigned pleasure in recording his belief that its discipline, energy, and devotion to the service could not have been surpassed.

3. From the beginning of November, when the troops were first put in motion, to the present time, every man has been employed in hard work, cheerfully performed, often under the most trying circumstances of heat and frost, always bivouacking on the mountain side, in rude huts of grass or leaves, officers and men sharing the same accommodation, marching day by day over precipitous mountains, rising at one time to six thousand feet, and having made a road fit for elephants from Luckipur to Chipowee, a distance of one hundred and three miles. The spirits of the troops never

flagged, and when they met the enemy, they drove them from their stockades and strongholds until they were glad to sue for mercy.

4. The history of the Expedition from first to last has been sheer hard work.

5. On the advance wings of the 22nd Regiment, Native Infantry, under Colonel Stafford, the 42nd Regiment, Native Infantry, under Colonel Rattray, C.S.I., and the 44th Regiment, Native Infantry, under Lieutenant-Colonel Nuthall, the hardest work has fallen. Each has shared in the actual fighting, the 44th more than either of the other corps, but to the officers in the rear most important duties were assigned in protecting a line of communication extending over one hundred and ten miles from Tipai Mukh to Volonel's stronghold of Chamfai, and watching through spies the attitude of the inhabitants of the neighbouring villages, conveying provisions and the post, and keeping the road constantly patrolled. The Frontier Police did equally good service with the troops in this way. Each field-officer in the rear had assigned to him a certain number of posts for which he was responsible, and to their vigilance may be attributed the fact that our communications have not for a day been interrupted.

6. Young officers may especially feel glad at having had such an opportunity of gaining experience in mountain warfare.

7. Before taking leave of the Column, the Brigadier-General would tender his heartfelt thanks to the officers, civil and military, non-commissioned officers and soldiers, who, for so many weeks, have co-operated with him, and to whom he feels he is entirely indebted for any success which may have attended the operations. He will have much pleasure in bringing their conduct, and that of the officers of the several departments, civil and military, with the Column, to the notice of His Excellency the Commander-in-Chief, for submission to the Government of India.

By Order, (Signed) H. THOMSON,
Captain Brigade-Major.

Notwithstanding the outcry raised both in Lushai and at home concerning the large scale on which the Expedition was conducted, and the loudly expressed remarks of those who know nothing about the subject, that a native regiment going in with a rush would effect all that was desired, we have seen that, after deducting the guards necessary at the various stations to keep open communications, only a force of four hundred men were available for the final advance on Chumfai, not by any means too many, supposing the Lushais had made a stand at Tulcheng, which it was not at all certain on leaving Chelam that they would not do.

The Expedition was carefully organised, and the steadiness and deliberation of the advance has probably had a greater effect on the Lushai mind than any sudden dash through a small portion of their hills could possibly have had, however successful it might have been in its immediate results.

As was the case in the Abyssinian Expedition, the prophesiers of evil were very numerous; fever, bronchitis, leeches, ticks, mosquitoes were among some of the many evils which would overtake us. The country was full of deep ravines whence escape was impossible, into which treacherous Lushais were to guide us, till suddenly an avalanche of rocks, loosened by our enemies from above, should annihilate the force; our coolies were to be destroyed along the line of communications, and any small detached parties would inevitably be cut off.

All these, and many more prophecies with which the Indian papers abounded, and which our friends who were not going with us repeated with infinite though suppressed delight, proved entirely false, and for my part I know I can answer for many others. I should not at all dislike another visit to that very fine country, always pre-supposing that I might make my own commissariat arrangements.

What the ultimate results may be of this last Expedition it is impossible at present to foretell. A road-making expedition has been sanctioned for the next cold weather, but the details as to the troops who will compose it, and the direction the road will take, are not generally known.

It is proposed to take the road through from

Cachar to Chittagong, by doing which, and also
by establishing a force at Tipai Mukh, it is hoped
to secure the objects of the Expedition by culti-
vating friendly relations with the Hill-men, and,
by opening up for them communications with
the plains, to give them an incentive to trade;
at the same time that, should future punishment
be necessary, we shall have an easy access into
their country.

THE END.